LEGACY SECURED EXIT

Table of Contents

thinkerz PUBLISHING

First published in Great Britain in 2025

Published by Thinkerz Publishing

www.thinkerz.co.uk

This book is not intended to provide personalised legal, financial, or investment advice. The author and publisher specifically disclaim any liability incurred as a consequence of the use and application of any content within.

Introduction

Who This Book Is For

- Business owners who've spent 20, 30, even 40 years building something real
- Founders quietly thinking about succession or stepping back
- People who care deeply about what happens to their staff, customers, and legacy
- Owners juggling the day-to-day while wrestling with how and when to exit
- Anyone looking for clarity, confidence, and a straight-talking plan to get out clean

You've put in the graft. This business has been your life's work. And now, the idea of stepping away feels... complicated. Emotional. Unclear. You're not interested in hype or theory — you want to know what to do, when to do it, and how to walk away with your head held high.

That's exactly what this book is built for.

Why You Can Trust What's in This Book

I've been in the trenches. Sold my first business without knowing what I didn't know — and I paid the price. Since then, I've made it my mission to understand this process inside out. I've advised owners, sellers, and successors across sectors — many with family dynamics and years of emotional investment tied in.

This isn't theory. It's the lived reality of guiding deals through messy transitions, protecting what matters most, and making sure no value gets left on the table. I don't do fluff. What I do offer is calm, straight-talking, battle-tested insight — shaped by decades of hard-won experience and grounded in integrity.

If you're looking for someone to help you exit with clarity, control, and confidence — you're in the right place.

Why I Wrote This Book

You've put your life into this business. And now you're staring down one of the biggest decisions you'll ever make: how to step away without losing everything you've built.

You're not just thinking about money — you're thinking about your people, your name, your legacy. You're juggling tough questions about timing, valuation, and what happens next. And deep down, you're worried that one wrong move could undo years of hard work.

I get it. I've been there. The weight of responsibility, the fear of regret, the endless second-guessing — I've felt all of it. That's why I wrote this book. To give you a straight-talking guide through the noise. So you can exit on your terms, with clarity, control, and peace of mind.

What You'll Get From This Book

A clear, honest view of what your business is really worth—and how to increase that value

A practical, step-by-step plan to exit smoothly, with your goals at the centre

Tools to tackle the legal, financial, and emotional complexities with confidence

Smart ways to reduce your tax bill and walk away with more in your pocket

Peace of mind knowing your people, your legacy, and your reputation are protected

This isn't fluff or theory. It's hard-won insight from someone who's lived it and helped others do the same. You'll walk away with clarity, direction, and a roadmap that's actually usable. No jargon. No guesswork. Just the real steps to help you exit well—and on your terms.

Your Step-by-Step Exit Roadmap

Personal Alignment – Get clear on why you're exiting, what life looks like after, and what really matters to you.

Robust Financials – Clean up and normalise your numbers, understand your true value, and build a financial story buyers will believe.

Independence Building – Shift reliance away from you. Strengthen your team, document your processes, and make your business stand on its own.

Market Positioning – Pinpoint what makes your business valuable, then package it to attract the right buyer at the right price.

Exit Readiness – Prepare the legal, tax, and emotional foundations so nothing gets missed—and nothing catches you off guard.

This is a practical framework that works. No theory, no fluff. Just a clear path forward that moves you from uncertainty to control—step by step, with confidence at every stage

CHAPTER 1: Planting Your Legacy

Legacy Is Planting Seeds in a Garden You Never Get to See

There's a quote often attributed to Greek philosophers that says:

"A society grows great when old men plant trees whose shade they know they shall never sit in."

That's what legacy really is.

It's not just what you build.

It's what you leave — for others to sit beneath, grow from, and carry forward.

As a business owner, your legacy is already in motion. Every decision you make, every hire, every customer interaction — they all shape what your business will become, with or without you.

But here's the uncomfortable truth:

If you don't plan that legacy with intention, you risk leaving behind confusion, pressure, or even resentment.

And that's not what any founder wants.

Legacy Isn't a Moment. It's a Series of Choices.

Too many owners think legacy is something that happens after they exit.

But legacy starts now — with how you lead, how you treat people, and how you prepare for your eventual transition.

It's in the systems you build.

The team you empower.

The culture you nurture.

And the plan you make for life beyond your leadership.

You don't have to know exactly when you'll exit. But you do need to know this:

Legacy doesn't happen by accident.

It happens by design.

The Silent Risk of Waiting Too Long

Here's where many owners unintentionally sabotage their legacy:

They wait.

They assume there will always be time to "sort it out later."

But life doesn't always wait. Health changes. Markets shift. Team members move on. And suddenly, the garden you spent years cultivating is left without a gardener — or worse, without a map.

That's when good businesses stall.

Cultures fray.

Values erode.

And the story you meant to leave behind gets rewritten by circumstances, not intention.

◈ "Legacy takes root before you leave."

What Legacy Could Look Like in Practice

Here are some quiet, powerful signals of a well-planted legacy:

• A leadership team that makes decisions with confidence — even when you're not in the room.

• A team that understands not just what to do, but why it matters.

• Customers who feel the same care and commitment they always have — even after your name is no longer on the signature line.

• Family members who feel clarity, not conflict, when it comes time for transition.

That's legacy.

Not just what you built — but what continues when you're gone.

Action Step: Write Your Legacy Line

Here's a quick but powerful exercise:

Write your legacy in one sentence. Not what you hope for — what you want to be remembered for.

Examples:

• "He built something great and left it better."

• "She empowered a team that kept growing without her."

• "They led with integrity and exited with grace."

Let that one sentence become a compass. A reminder. A filter for the decisions you make from here on out.

Final Thought

You may not sit in the shade of the tree you're planting.

But someone will.

Your team. Your clients. Your family. Even your future self.

And when that day comes — when the garden grows in your absence — let it be strong, rooted, and full of life.

Because that's what legacy is:

The result of a thousand thoughtful seeds, planted while no one was watching — and remembered long after you've stepped away.

"What seeds are you planting today that someone else will benefit from tomorrow?"

The hidden risks, regrets, and ripple effects of exit procrastination

Let's be real for a second.

Most business owners don't avoid exit planning because they're lazy.

They avoid it because it's overwhelming, emotional — and sometimes, existential.

So they push it back:

"I'll think about that next quarter."

"Let's wait until the next milestone."

"I'm not ready yet. Maybe in a few years."

And just like that... another year passes.

But here's the truth: **doing nothing is still a decision.** And it's one that comes with a cost — not just financial, but personal, emotional, and relational.

Procrastination Is Expensive

When you delay exit planning:

- Your business becomes more reliant on you
- Operational cracks deepen without resolution
- Staff uncertainty grows (even if they don't say it out loud)
- Buyers perceive higher risk and reduce offers
- You lose your own mental, emotional, and physical readiness window

I've seen owners lose hundreds of thousands — not because the business wasn't strong, but because the timing was wrong. They weren't prepared, and they didn't have options when it counted.

The Risk of a Forced Exit

You never think it'll be you — until it is:

- A health scare derails everything
- A key staff member leaves unexpectedly
- A buyer appears, but the business isn't ready
- Or... you simply burn out and lose the passion to lead

Without a clear plan, these moments turn into chaos.

Even worse?

Many owners end up selling from fatigue, not strength. Or worse — closing the doors entirely.

That's not an exit. That's an emotional surrender.

Legacy or Liability?

Here's the uncomfortable part:

If you don't plan your exit, you may unintentionally **leave behind a burden** — for your team, your family, or your community.

A few of the downstream consequences I've seen:

- A strong business sells for a weak price

- Family conflict erupts over unclear intentions
- Buyers walk away after discovering hidden issues
- Staff leave because they don't know what's next
- The business folds — not from lack of value, but lack of readiness

Your business isn't just a balance sheet. It's a story. A team. A culture.

Planning protects all of it.

Clarity Comes From Action

You don't need all the answers right now.

But you do need to **start**.

Because when you take action — even small steps — things get clearer.

Your stress goes down. Your decisions get better.

And you give yourself options instead of pressure.

This isn't about locking in a date.

It's about **building optionality** — so you can exit when you're ready, not when you're forced.

Action Steps: How to Break the Stalemate

Here's where to begin — without overwhelm:

1. **Take 30 minutes and reflect**What would a peaceful, purposeful exit look like for you?
2. **Identify 1 hidden risk**(e.g. client concentration, owner

dependency, unclear succession)

3. **Block one hour next week**Use it to document something: your vision, your goals, or your team plan.
4. **Have one meaningful conversation**Talk to your advisor, spouse, or key team member. Bring them in early.

The Clock Doesn't Stop — But You Can Catch Up

Every owner I've worked with says the same thing:

"I wish I'd started this sooner."

Don't let that be your story too.

You don't need to rush. But you do need to prepare.

Because when the moment comes, you want to be leading it — not reacting to it.

Your future deserves more than procrastination.

And your legacy is too valuable to be left to chance.

The Exit Clock: When Is the Right Time to Start?

One of the questions I get asked most often by business owners is:

"When should I start planning my exit?"

And my answer is always the same:

Sooner than you think.

The exit clock doesn't start ticking when you're ready to retire — it starts now.

Not because you're heading out the door tomorrow, but because planning early gives you something that last-minute deals never do: control.

When you get ahead of it, you get to shape your future on your terms — not under pressure from burnout, a health scare, family shifts, or a surprise offer that catches you off guard.**Planning Early Doesn't Mean You're Quitting**

Let's clear something up.

Early planning doesn't mean you're leaving the business tomorrow. Far from it.

Some of the smoothest, most profitable exits I've seen took two to five years to pull off — because the owner had the foresight to start early, without pressure. They created space to think clearly, reduce stress, and shape both the business and their own future.

Think of it like selling your house. You don't wait until the buyer's outside with a van before you fix the broken door or repaint the living room. You prepare it, so when the right moment comes, you're ready — and the value reflects that effort.

It's the same with your business.**See Your Business Through a Buyer's Eyes**

Here's the reality check:

Your business isn't worth what you feel it's worth. It's worth what someone is willing to pay.

Buyers aren't just looking at your profits — they're looking at risk.

Is everything dependent on you? Are there gaps in your leadership team? Are your financials clear and up to date?

That's why early planning should include an objective valuation — not through your lens, but through the buyer's. The sooner you understand what they'll see, the sooner you can address the issues that could hurt value.

And the upside? Fixing those things doesn't just increase value — it makes your life easier too.**Let Your Life Goals Shape the Timeline**

Exit planning isn't just about spreadsheets and share price. It's about life.

Before you start prepping the business, take a moment to reflect on yourself.

- What do you want your next chapter to look like?
- How much involvement do you want after the sale?
- What kind of buyer would you feel good handing the keys to?

The answers to those questions shape your timeline — not the other way around.

Because it's not just about when the business is ready. It's about when you are.**Build a Business That Works Without You**

One of the biggest levers of value is this:

Can the business run without you?

If you're still the go-to for every major decision, that's a red flag for buyers.

The more you build independence into the business, the more attractive it becomes.

Start now:

- Delegate decisions
- Document key processes
- Mentor a leadership team
- Let others take ownership of big projects

You'll boost value and free yourself to think more strategically.**Don't Forget the Emotional Side**

Exiting a business isn't just a financial event — it's an emotional one.

You've built something meaningful. Letting go is never easy.

Early planning gives you space to process the shift. To ease into the next chapter, not fall into it. And to make peace with the change long before it happens.

Because the worst exits I've seen?

They weren't about low valuations. They were about owners who weren't emotionally ready.**Stay Sharp on the Numbers**

Clean, current, accurate financials are a gift — for you and your buyer.

Keep them updated. Track the right KPIs. Understand your cash flow.

This isn't just good practice — it makes you exit-ready at any moment.**Time Is Your Advantage**

So when should you start planning?

Right now.

Because when the time comes — whether it's in two years or ten — you want to be ready.

Not scrambling. Not guessing. Not settling.

Planning now means you're prepared later.

And that's a win no matter when the clock runs out.

"If you had to exit 12 months from today, what would you panic about most?"

What Makes a Business Valuable (and What Hurts It)

When people talk about what makes a business valuable, they usually go straight to the obvious stuff:Turnover.

Profit.

Customer numbers.

How busy it is.

But here's the truth most owners miss: buyers aren't buying "busy."

They're buying **stability, transferability, and future cash flow**.

And that means the things that truly drive value might not be what you think.

This chapter breaks it down — simply, honestly — so you can focus on what really matters.

	What Hurts Value
Transferable, recurring revenue	Owner-dependence
Strong middle management	Customer concentration
Clean, normalised financials	Outdated systems
Cultural continuity	No succession plan

1. Transferable Revenue > Temporary Wins

You might have just had your best year ever — but if that revenue came from a one-off deal, or it disappears the moment you do, it holds little weight with buyers.

What buyers love:

- Recurring or contracted revenue
- Diverse customer base
- Predictable cash flow
- Minimal concentration risk

◈ **Quick Win**: Map out where your revenue comes from. If more than 20% comes from one client or one-off jobs, that's a flag — and an opportunity.**2. You (The Owner) Shouldn't Be the Business**

This one's tough to hear, but essential:

The more your business depends on you, the less it's worth.

Buyers don't want to buy your energy. They want to buy a machine that works **without** you.

If you're the key decision-maker, relationship holder, and daily problem-solver — that's risk, not value.

◈ **Quick Win**: Start documenting how things run. What happens if you take two weeks off? What breaks? Fix those gaps first.**3. Strong Financials = Strong Confidence**

Buyers don't just look at revenue. They look under the hood.

Margins. Adjustments. Seasonality. Working capital needs.

Most importantly, they want to see **clean, credible, and consistent numbers** — not a mystery they have to decode.

What matters:

• Normalised EBITDA

• Cash flow stability

• Clean financial records

• Separation of personal costs

• Visibility of CapEx and operational gearing

◈ **Quick Win**: Get a simple, buyer-focused valuation done — not just to get a number, but to understand what's helping and hurting value.**4. Team Strength Drives Buyer Confidence**

A capable team is one of the most overlooked value drivers.

It signals resilience, stability, and growth potential.

Buyers ask:

• Who makes the business run?

• Who stays when the owner leaves?

• Can the team scale this without hand-holding?

If the answer is "just the owner," that's a red flag.

If there's leadership depth, that's a win.

◈ **Quick Win**: Review your org chart. Who's critical? Who's replaceable? Start cross-training or mentoring now to plug succession gaps.**5. Culture Is Quiet Value — But Real**

Culture doesn't show up on a balance sheet — but it shows up in retention, stability, morale, and buyer impressions.

If your team believes in the business...

If your clients feel looked after...

If people stick around...

That's real value — because it makes everything easier to transfer.

◈ **Quick Win**: Write down your company values. Not slogans — actual behaviours. Use them to reinforce culture, guide hires, and help buyers understand what makes your business tick.**6. Real Value vs. Perceived Success**

Some businesses look strong on the surface — big turnover, shiny brand, lots of activity.

But dig deeper, and it's chaos:

Thin margins

Owner burnout

No systems

Meanwhile, some quietly run gems — modest in size but clean, steady, and low-risk — sell for strong multiples.

Don't confuse "busy" with "valuable."

Don't undervalue "boring" if it's stable and transferable.

◈ **Quick Win**: Ask an external advisor: "What would worry you about my business if you were the buyer?" Listen carefully.**Closing Thought: Think Like a Buyer**

The more you think like a buyer, the better decisions you'll make now.

They're not buying your history.

They're buying the future — and the confidence that comes with it.

So build that future now:

- Simplify your revenue
- Systemise your operations
- Empower your team
- Clean up your numbers
- Reinforce your culture

Because value isn't found in the fluff — it's in the foundations.

Your Exit Is Not a Transaction — It's a Transformation

Let's clear up one of the biggest myths around selling your business:

It's all about the money.

It's not.

Yes, financials matter. You want a solid valuation, clean numbers, good terms.

But a true exit — the kind that gives you peace of mind and preserves what you've built — isn't just about the deal.

It's about transformation.

Because exiting a business isn't just a financial milestone.

It's a shift in role.

A change in identity.

A redefinition of what life looks like — for you, for your team, and for the business itself.

You're not just transferring shares.

You're stepping into a whole new chapter.**More Than a Cheque — This Is Personal**

Selling a house is a transaction.

Selling a business? That's emotional.

You've poured your energy, time, and talent into something real.

You've built relationships, weathered storms, celebrated wins.

So when it comes time to let go — even partly — it's never just "sign here and move on."

And when you treat it like just another business deal? That's when regrets creep in.

Because you didn't just sell a company — you closed a chapter of your life.**Start With Alignment**

Ask any owner who's rushed their exit, and many will say the same thing:

"It didn't feel right."

Why? Because the exit wasn't aligned.

It wasn't built around who they are or what they wanted next.

A meaningful exit starts with clarity. Not just financial clarity — **personal clarity**.

- Do you want freedom and time? Or to stay involved in a mentoring role?
- Do you want to pass it on to family? Or sell to someone who'll scale it?
- Do you want a clean break? Or a phased step back?

There's no right answer. But there is your answer.

And the sooner you define it, the smoother the path forward becomes.**Design the Exit — Don't Drift Into It**

Great exits don't happen by luck.

They're built over time, with intention.

They include:

- Succession planning
- Systemising operations
- Reducing reliance on the owner
- Emotional preparation
- Culture preservation
- Buyer fit

And yes, tax planning and financial readiness too.

If that feels like a lot — it is. But you don't need to do it all at once.

You just need to start.**Value Goes Beyond the Number**

Let's be real: the money matters.

You've earned it.

But real value isn't just what ends up in your bank account.

It's also:

- Whether your team thrives after you
- Whether the brand continues to stand for something

- Whether your clients stay well-served
- Whether you feel proud, clear, and at peace

That's what happens when you exit with meaning — not just money.**What a Transformation-Focused Exit Looks Like**

When you approach your exit as a transformation:

⟐ You don't just sell — you prepare the business for life without you

⟐ You don't just talk numbers — you show systems, leadership, and resilience

⟐ You don't just hand it over — you guide the next chapter

⟐ You don't just leave — you lead

It's not about perfection. It's about intention.**Action Steps to Begin**

⟐ **1. Visualise Life After the Exit**

Get clear on what you want next — this becomes your North Star.

⟐ **2. Check Your Emotional Readiness**

Are you still clinging to control? Or are you ready to let others lead?

⟐ **3. Strengthen Operational Independence**

Document your systems. Delegate. Let your team stretch their wings.

⟐ **4. Get a Valuation That Tells a Story**

Not just numbers — but context. What's strong? What's risky? Fix what you can.

◈ 5. Map the Transition

Outline your exit timeline, ideal buyer traits, and how you'll support the shift.

◈ 6. Protect Culture

What values do you want to last? Codify them. Embed them. Lead by example.**The Way You Exit Becomes the Way You're Remembered**

No one will remember your last invoice.

But they will remember how you exited.

- Did you leave a mess? Or a legacy?
- Did you walk away quietly? Or with clarity and grace?
- Did the business survive? Or thrive without you?

This is your final act as the leader.

Write it well. Own it fully.

Because when you exit as a transformation — not just a transaction —

you don't just close a chapter.

You finish the book with pride.

"You're not just walking away from a business — you're stepping into a new version of your life. This isn't the end of the story. It's the part they'll remember."

CHAPTER 2: Defining Success — Personal Alignment Before the Deal

The Emotional Side of Exit No One Talks About

Let's have a real conversation.

When business owners talk about exit, the focus tends to go straight to the numbers.

Valuation. Multiples. Deal structure. Tax.

And all of that matters. Of course it does.

But there's a deeper layer — the one that rarely gets airtime:

The emotional side.

And if we ignore it, we risk undermining everything we've worked so hard to build.

Because exiting a business isn't just a transaction.

It's a transition. A transformation. A shift in identity.You're Not Just Selling a Business — You're Letting Go of a Life Chapter

For most founders, the business is more than a job or an asset.

It's your rhythm. Your purpose. Your reason to keep going during the hard times.

It's where you found confidence.

Where you earned your scars.

Where you made decisions that shaped not just your career — but your character.

So when the time comes to exit, it's not as simple as signing paperwork.

It can feel like stepping off a moving train. Like handing over part of yourself.

And the question that surfaces — quietly, but persistently — is:

"Who am I without this?"

That's not weakness. That's being human.

And the key isn't to ignore it. It's to work through it with awareness and care.**Guilt and Loyalty Go Hand in Hand**

If you've built a tight-knit team, exit can stir guilt.

Guilt about leaving them behind.

Guilt about selling to someone who might change the culture.

Guilt about the unknown.

It's common — and heavy. You've likely carried your team for years.

You've felt responsible for not just paychecks, but futures.

But here's the reframe:

Taking care of yourself is not a betrayal.

If you exit with thoughtfulness, integrity, and transparency — you model leadership to the very end.

And that's a legacy your team will remember.**Even When the Numbers Make Sense... Fear Creeps In**

You might have the valuation you wanted.

The buyer's solid. The terms are fair.

And yet — you hesitate.

Why?

Because fear doesn't care about spreadsheets.

Fear whispers:

"What if I regret this?"

"What if the business collapses without me?"

"What if I feel lost?"

These aren't red flags — they're normal.

You don't beat fear with more data.

You beat it with preparation.Emotional Readiness Is Exit Readiness

Most advisors will help you sort the financials, legal docs, and timelines.

But the emotional side? That's on you.

And if you skip it — you risk sabotaging the deal or regretting it later.

This is where the real work begins.Action Steps: Prepare Your Mind, Not Just Your Business

1. Redefine Your Identity

Ask: Who am I beyond the business?

List the roles you're excited to step into next. Think beyond the exit.

2. Visualise Post-Exit Life

What does a meaningful day look like for you — without the business?

Think purpose. People. Projects. Not just downtime.

3. Write a Letter to Your Team

Even if you never send it, write what you'd say to them if you were leaving tomorrow.

It helps process the emotional layers of letting go.

4. Talk to Your Inner Circle

Bring your family into the conversation. Share your fears. Ask for their perspective.

This isn't just your transition — it affects them too.

5. Build Emotional Support

Don't go it alone. Talk to a coach, a mentor, or another exited founder.

Sometimes, just being heard is enough to create clarity.**There's No "Right" Emotion — Only Real Ones**

Some owners feel relief. Some feel grief.

Some feel both at once.

What matters isn't how you feel — it's that you're honest about it.

Because the more emotionally prepared you are, the smoother your exit will be — not just on the surface, but deep down where it counts.**Your Emotional Legacy Is Just as Important as the Financial One**

People won't remember the headline number.

They'll remember how you made them feel.

How you exited. How you led.

So make it intentional. Make it graceful.

Make it human.

Because yes — the money matters.

But the way you leave?

That's what lasts.

Quick Reflection: Am I Emotionally Ready?

- Have I thought about who I'll be after the business?
- Can I imagine life without the business title?
- Am I excited, nervous, or avoidant — and why?

Tony Robbins said it well:

"Success without fulfillment is the ultimate failure."

And nowhere does that ring louder than in the context of exiting a business.

Because when most people talk about a "successful exit," they're usually thinking about one thing:

The cheque.

What's the multiple? What's the walkaway figure? How much did they "get"?

But here's the part nobody talks about in most deal rooms:

If the exit doesn't feel right, no amount of money will make it satisfying.

You might cash out — but inside, something stays unsettled.

Because a true exit isn't just about what you get.

It's about what you leave behind. And how you feel when you walk away.

It's Not Just a Sale — It's a Shift in Identity

You didn't build your business for a payout.

You built it for freedom. For purpose. For family. For something to call your own.

You built it in your way, on your terms, with your values stitched into the culture.

So when it's time to step away, it's not just about numbers.

It's emotional.

It's identity.

It's legacy.

And when those elements are ignored — when the process becomes purely transactional — you can end up financially rich but personally empty.

That's not just disappointing.

That's the kind of success that feels like failure.

Legacy Over Liquidity

Let's be clear: price matters.

You deserve to get paid for what you've built.

But value isn't always measured in pounds and pence.

I've seen owners walk away from seven-figure deals — not because the number was wrong, but because the feeling was.

They didn't trust the buyer.

They weren't confident the culture would survive.

They weren't ready to let go in that way.

They made the right call.

Because legacy beats liquidity — every time.

Alignment First, Always

A fulfilling exit is one where your values, your vision, and your future all align.

Ask yourself:

- What will this business stand for after I'm gone?
- What matters more: the number on the cheque — or the story I leave behind?
- How will I feel when it's no longer mine?

These aren't abstract questions. They're core.

If you don't get clear on them, your exit risks becoming reactive and regretful.

With clarity?

Your exit becomes intentional — and powerful.

Plan the Person, Not Just the Price

Exit planning isn't just spreadsheets and timelines.

It's emotional navigation.

It's asking:

- Who am I when I'm not the owner anymore?
- What will my days look like?
- What will give me purpose?

Most owners don't struggle with selling.

They struggle with what comes after.

So don't wait for the silence to hit. Prepare now.

🔷 **Action Step:** Visualise your post-exit life. Not a fantasy — a real week. What fills your time? What excites you? What restores your energy?

If you don't know yet, it's a sign to pause — not push.

Your Team Is Part of the Story Too

The people you've led — they matter.

The culture you built.

The values you lived.

The way you showed up.

That's the emotional legacy.

🔷 **Action Step:** Write a letter to your team or your family. Capture what the journey meant to you — and what you hope lives on. Don't send it yet. Just write it for you.

Fulfillment Is the Real Finish Line

You can always make more money.

You can't always rebuild peace of mind.

A meaningful exit is one where you leave with your head high, your values intact, and your heart full.

That's the true win.

Not just "I got paid."

But "I left well. I exited with grace. I honoured what I built."

Final Thought

Don't just sell.

Align.

Exit on your terms — not just financially, but personally.

Because if you walk away rich but restless, you haven't exited.

You've escaped.

And your journey deserves a better ending than that.

Plan with heart. Lead with intention.

Because success without fulfillment... isn't success at all.

"So how do you avoid that quiet emptiness after the cheque clears? You get clear—before the deal begins."

Getting Clear on What You Really Want

Let's pause for a moment and ask the question that sits underneath everything in this book:

What do you really want?

Not what your accountant says.

Not what the market expects.

Not what your peers think you should aim for.

You. What do you **want?**

Because if your exit plan isn't built on what truly matters to you — what brings peace, purpose, and fulfillment — then what's the point?

Too many business owners chase someone else's version of success:

The big number. The quick sale. The flashy finish.

And then? They're left wondering why it all feels a little... empty.

So before we get into deals and documents, we need to get into something deeper: **clarity.**

Clarity Isn't a Luxury — It's the Foundation

Clarity doesn't come from financial models.

It comes from reflection.

From asking honest questions.

From slowing down long enough to tune into what actually matters to you.

From giving yourself permission to choose your path — not follow someone else's.

Because without clarity, you'll drift into a decision you may later regret.

With clarity? You move with purpose.

◈ **Action Step:** Write down what your version of a successful exit looks like. One sentence. Stick it somewhere visible. Let it guide your next move.

Wants vs. Needs — Spot the Difference

It's easy to get caught in the "wants":

- A certain sale price
- A clean break
- A bit of recognition

But underneath that? There are needs:

- Peace of mind
- Purpose beyond the business
- Trust that your team will be okay

Getting clear means being honest with yourself.

◈ **Action Step:** Write down three things you want from your exit. Then write three things you need. Notice the difference — and which ones really matter.

Know Your Core Values — And Honour Them

You've built your business on a certain set of values — whether written down or not.

So ask yourself:

Will your exit reflect those values?

If you care about people, don't sell to someone who'll treat your team like numbers.

If you value craftsmanship, don't hand it to someone who only sees margins.

If you've led with integrity, finish the same way.

◈ **Action Step:** Identify your top 3 values. Use them as a filter for all exit-related decisions — from buyer fit to deal structure.

Imagine Life After Exit — Don't Leave It Blank

One of the biggest mistakes owners make is seeing the exit as the finish line.

It's not. It's a doorway.

But if you haven't thought about what comes after — the space can feel empty.

That's when regret creeps in.

🔷 **Action Step:** Journal what your ideal post-exit week looks like. Not just the dream stuff — the real, everyday life stuff. What makes you feel alive? Energised? Useful?

Check In With Yourself — Regularly

Clarity isn't a one-off task. Life changes. So do priorities.

The version of success that felt right 5 years ago might not fit today.

That's okay — what matters is staying connected to what's true now.

🔷 **Action Step:** Block 30 minutes once a month for a "Clarity Check-In." Ask yourself: Am I still heading in the right direction? Adjust if needed.

Final Thought

This chapter might not feel urgent. But it's essential.

Because without clarity, you'll make decisions based on noise, pressure, or fear.

With clarity, you'll make decisions that feel right.

So take the time to get clear.

Define success on your own terms.

Let purpose lead, not just profit.

Because the best exits aren't just well-paid — they're well-aligned.

And that starts by knowing what you really want.

Write Your Exit Statement

"My definition of a successful exit is..."

"After I leave, I want to feel..."

"The life I want after exit looks like..."

Harvard Business Review said it best:

"Exiting a business is not just a financial transaction. It's a personal transformation — and often, an emotional reckoning."

And they're absolutely right.

Because behind every buyer conversation, valuation spreadsheet, and due diligence checklist... there's a person.

A founder.

An owner.

Someone who poured years — sometimes decades — of energy, identity, and sacrifice into building something that mattered.

Yes, selling your business is a financial event. But if we're being honest, it's emotional first.

And if you don't prepare for that part, it can blindside you — and it's often what leaves the deepest scars.**It's Not Just Business — It's Personal**

Let's get real: your business isn't "just a business."

It's the place you proved yourself.

Took risks.

Stayed up at night thinking.

Felt alivc — and sometimes crushed.

It's likely where your confidence, community, and even your sense of self came from.

So when you talk about stepping back, selling, or passing the baton — of course it stirs emotion.

That's not weakness. That's being human.

But in most exit planning advice, the emotional layer barely gets a mention.

And yet, it's often the most powerful driver — for better or worse.**Unspoken Emotions Shape Outcomes**

Here's what I've seen far too often:

- The deal is solid... but the owner pulls away.
- The buyer's strong... but the gut says no.
- The exit is close... but something feels off.

These hesitations don't come from the numbers — they come from unprocessed emotion.

Fear.

Guilt.

Loss.

Uncertainty.

Even grief.

And if you don't face those feelings early, they can cloud your judgement, stall your progress, or leave you with regrets long after the ink has dried.

"Legacy isn't just what you leave behind — it's how people feel when you're no longer in the room."**Start With Clarity: What's Really Driving This?**

Before you get tactical, you need to get personal.

Why are you exiting?

What are you moving toward — not just away from?

What does "success" feel like, not just look like?

Because the clearer you are on your "why," the more aligned your decisions become — and the more peace you'll feel during the process.

◈ **Action Step:** Write your own "Why I'm exiting" statement. Go beyond numbers. Think freedom, impact, peace, contribution — whatever feels true for you.**Emotional Waves Will Hit — Plan for Them**

The fear of losing relevance.

The guilt of "abandoning" your team.

The doubt that the buyer will protect what you built.

The sadness of letting go.

You won't see them coming all at once — but they'll hit.

And that's okay.

The goal isn't to eliminate these feelings. It's to expect them. To talk about them. To build room for them into your planning process.

� **Action Step:** Give your emotions space. Journal. Walk. Talk. Create a safe outlet — because pushing it down only makes it louder later.**Share the Emotional Load**

You don't have to do this solo. In fact, you shouldn't.

Bring your partner into the conversation.

Speak with your leadership team.

Find an advisor who understands the human side of selling.

People won't get in your way when they understand your "why." They'll help carry the weight.

� **Action Step:** Choose one person this week — spouse, advisor, business partner — and start the conversation. Share where you're at. Let them in.**Vision Lightens the Load**

The more clearly you can picture life after the business, the easier it becomes to let go.

Because when you don't know what's next, it's natural to cling to what's familiar — even if it no longer serves you.

� **Action Step:** Sketch out your ideal post-exit week. What would you do on Monday? Where would your energy go? What lights you up beyond work?**A Great Exit Feels Right — Not Just Pays Well**

In the end, you don't want to walk away just paid.

You want to walk away proud.

That's not just a financial achievement.

It's an emotional one.

Lead your exit with the same care, intention, and integrity you brought to building your business.

Because the emotional side isn't something to "manage."

It's where your truth lives.

And when you honour that — your exit won't just work on paper.

It'll feel right in your heart too.

Here's something you won't find in most spreadsheets, calculators, or even in the fine print of a deal sheet:

Emotional readiness — not financial readiness — is the #1 predictor of post-exit satisfaction.

That might sound surprising, especially if you're someone who's spent a career tracking revenue, chasing EBITDA, and negotiating terms. But I've seen it too many times to ignore.

The sale completes.

The money lands.

The numbers make sense...

And yet — something's off.

Because while the business was ready to exit... the owner wasn't.

Red Flag Indicators of Low Emotional Readiness

- Constantly delaying planning
- Conflicted about buyer offers that make sense on paper
- No clear answer to "What will you do next?"

What Most Exit Plans Miss

We spend years fine-tuning the numbers.

Margins. Growth. Forecasts. Tax strategy. Deal structure.

But very few owners stop to ask:

- Am I emotionally ready to let go?
- What will my life look like afterward?
- Who will I be when I'm no longer "the boss"?

And if you haven't asked those questions, your deal might close — but your peace won't arrive.

Because financial success without emotional alignment often leads to something quietly devastating: regret.**What Emotional Readiness Really Means**

Being emotionally ready doesn't mean you've got everything figured out.

It means you've paused long enough to get clear.

It means you understand:

- Why you're exiting
- What you're walking toward — not just away from
- What will bring you fulfilment in the next season
- How to navigate the identity shift that's coming

It's being able to look yourself in the mirror and say, "This feels right, not just logical."**The Identity Gap Hits Hard**

For many founders, their business has been more than a job.

It's been a source of identity, structure, and significance.

You've been the one people turn to.

You've had purpose baked into your routine.

Your name's been on the lease — and on the line.

So when that disappears, even if you've planned for it, it can feel like a part of you is being amputated.

If that gap isn't acknowledged — or worse, ignored — it becomes a void.

And no payout fills a void.**Get Clear on the Real Why**

Let's drop the mask for a minute.

Why do you really want to exit?

Are you burned out?

Are you craving freedom?

Is something shifting in your family or health?

Is there a deeper calling pulling at you?

There's no shame in any answer — only wisdom in knowing it.

◈ **Action Step:** Ask yourself "Why now?" — then ask it again. Peel back the layers until you land on something honest, even if it's messy. That's where your real clarity lives.**Create a Vision That Pulls You Forward**

A smooth exit needs more than clean numbers — it needs a compelling next chapter.

What does life look like on the other side?

Not just the first few weeks of rest — but the rhythm of a meaningful life.

• What will get you out of bed?

• Who do you want to spend time with?

• What gives you energy and purpose?

◈ **Action Step:** Sketch your ideal post-exit week. No filters. What's Monday morning like? What are you doing at 11am? What's your new "win" for the day?

If you can't picture life after the sale, you'll struggle to let go of the life you've known.**Build Your Emotional Advisory Circle**

Exit planning isn't just for lawyers and accountants.

You need someone who'll walk with you — the person, not just the owner.

That might be a mentor, coach, therapist, or another exited founder.

Someone who'll tell you the truth.

Who gets it.

Who can hold space when things feel uncertain.

◈ **Action Step:** Choose one person you trust to be your sounding board. Not for strategy — for you. Let them into your process.**Final Thought: It's Not Just About Getting Out — It's About Moving On**

You've built something meaningful.

Now, the next chapter isn't just about closing the deal — it's about opening your life.

So yes — sort the numbers, clean the books, structure the deal.

But don't forget the inner work.

Because when the final wire lands and the noise dies down, what really matters is whether you can say,

"This feels right. I'm ready. Let's go."

That's not just a clean exit.

That's a fulfilled one.

And that's the kind that lasts.

"Financial readiness may win the deal — but emotional readiness determines if you'll regret it."

Freedom on Your Terms: Redefining What Success Really Means

Let's get to the heart of it.

Success is only success if it actually feels like freedom — not just in your calendar, but in your chest.

But too many business owners end up chasing a version of success that was never really theirs to begin with. Big numbers. Big headlines. The kind of sale that looks impressive on LinkedIn — but quietly leaves you feeling... flat.

Here's what most don't realise until it's too late:

You get to define what success looks like.

You get to choose what freedom means to you.

And when your exit is shaped around that — everything changes.

You stop chasing.

You start choosing.

You lead with clarity, not comparison.**Are You Chasing the Wrong Finish Line?**

It's a hard question, but an important one:

Whose version of success have you been chasing?

Was it inherited?

Driven by ego?

Fueled by competition or comparison?

Or was it built on your values — on peace, purpose, time with your family, contribution, meaning?

Because here's the truth:

You can exit with millions and still feel empty if it's not aligned with what you actually want.**What Freedom Really Looks Like**

Freedom isn't a yacht.

It's not early retirement unless you want it to be.

It's not about escaping — it's about arriving.

For some, freedom is adventure.

For others, it's stillness.

It might be mentoring. Or writing. Or spending real time with the people you love without always checking your phone.

Whatever your version is — **own it**.

◇ **Action Step:** Write one sentence that defines what freedom means to you. Keep it where you'll see it every day as you plan your exit.**Success = Freedom + Legacy**

Freedom is one half of the equation.

The other half? Legacy.

Because if you've built something meaningful, you probably don't just want to walk away — you want to leave it in good hands.

That means:

- A business that thrives without you
- A culture that lives on
- A team that feels proud to carry it forward

Legacy is the emotional return on everything you've poured into the business.

🔘 **Action Step:** Ask yourself: "What do I want people to say about the business — and about me — one year after I've stepped back?"**Freedom Without a Plan is Just Wishful Thinking**

Let's get practical.

True freedom comes from structure — not chaos.

That means building a transition that supports your goals, values, and peace of mind.

You'll need:

- Clean financials
- Operational systems that run without you
- A leadership team that can step up
- A post-exit vision that excites you

🔘 **Action Step:** Build your own "Freedom Framework." What has to be true — financially, emotionally, operationally — for you to walk away with confidence?**What Will You Grow Into?**

Here's something most owners don't expect:

Freedom can feel unsettling.

The business has been your compass for years. So when it's gone, you need something new to point toward.

That's where growth comes in — not just for the business, but for you.

Try something new.

Travel. Mentor. Heal. Explore.

Or just... be still, and see what rises.

◇ **Action Step:** Create a "next chapter" list. Not goals — just ideas. Possibilities that feel expansive, even if you're not ready to act on them yet.**The Final Question**

Success is not just about what you walk away with.

It's about what you walk away to.

So ask yourself:

- What does freedom mean to me now?
- What legacy do I want to leave?
- How do I want to feel when I step away?

Let those answers guide your exit.

Because when you define success on your terms —

you don't just exit.

You evolve.

And that's a win that can't be measured in multiples.

"There's no right version of success — only yours."

How to Separate Your Identity from Your Business

Let's be real for a moment.

When you've built something from scratch — poured in the energy, late nights, resilience, and sacrifices — it stops being just a business.

It becomes you.

And that's where things get complicated. Because the tighter your identity is wrapped around the business, the harder it becomes to imagine a life beyond it — even when you know it's time to exit.

The truth? For many founders, the toughest part of letting go isn't financial.

It's personal.

It's the quiet question that lingers beneath all the spreadsheets and planning:

Who am I without this?

If that question hits you in the chest... good. You're not alone. And you're asking the right question.**You Are Not Your Business**

Let's start here: your business is something you built.

It's not who you are.

You are not your P&L.

You are not your team size.

You are not your client list or your turnover.

You're a whole human — with a life beyond invoices, strategy meetings, and the constant hum of being "the boss."

But when you've spent years being the glue that holds everything together, it's easy to forget that you existed before the business — and you'll still exist after.

◈ **Action Step:** Write down five things that define you outside of your business. Use them as a reminder: I am more than my company.**Step 1: Reconnect with the Person Behind the Business**

Ask yourself:

• What brings me joy that has nothing to do with work?

• What did I love doing before this business?

• What parts of me have been put on hold?

This isn't about hobbies for the sake of hobbies. It's about reconnecting with who you are underneath the title.

◈ **Action Step:** Start a "me list" — interests, people, places, and activities that make you feel alive. Then schedule one into your week.**Step 2: Create Breathing Space**

When the business is your life, everything else shrinks. Relationships, health, creativity — they all get crowded out.

It's time to make space again.

• Reclaim evenings and weekends

• Switch off without guilt

- Take a full day away from operations — and let the team lead
- Say yes to something you'd normally postpone

This isn't self-indulgent. It's vital preparation for life beyond your exit.

◈ **Action Step:** Block out one full "non-business" day this month. Use it to recharge you, not just your to-do list.**Step 3: Let Others Lead**

Control and identity often go hand in hand.

"If I'm not making the calls, am I still valuable?"

But here's the irony: the more your business relies on you, the harder it is to leave — and the more your identity stays trapped in your role.

Empower your team.

Document your systems.

Train successors.

Let go of tasks that drain you.

The more independent the business becomes, the more space you create for a new version of yourself to emerge.

◈ **Action Step:** Choose one area where you're the bottleneck. Hand it over. Fully. No strings attached.**Step 4: Build a Post-Exit Vision That's About You**

You can't step into something new if you don't know what it is.

That's why identity transition is just as important as succession planning.

Ask:

- What do I want my days to look like after exit?
- How do I want to feel?
- What do I want to build, explore, or contribute to next?

This isn't fluff. It's the foundation for your next chapter.

◈ **Action Step:** Visualise one week in your post-exit life. Monday to Sunday. Write it out. Let that guide your exit plan, not just the financials.

Ways to Reclaim Yourself Beyond the Business

- Say yes to one non-business activity weekly
- Introduce yourself without your title
- Reconnect with parts of your life you've put on hold

Final Thought: The Business Was a Chapter — Not the Whole Book

You're not just a founder. You're not just a CEO.

You're a full human being — with depth, dreams, and value far beyond the company you built.

Exiting the business isn't about walking away from who you are.

It's about returning to who you've always been.

So as you plan your exit, plan your reinvention too.

Not just what you're leaving — but what you're walking toward.

Because the most important thing you'll ever lead... is yourself.

"Once you remember who you are outside the business, you're ready to shape what you leave behind..."

What Legacy Means — And How to Protect Yours

When most people talk about exiting a business, the spotlight's on the numbers.

Revenue. EBITDA. Multiples. Terms.

And yes — those things matter. You deserve to realise the value you've built.

But if you're like most founders I've worked with, there's more to it than just money.

You care about the people.

The culture.

The name you've spent years shaping.

The story behind the spreadsheets.

That's legacy.

And here's the truth: legacy doesn't magically appear when you sign the deal.

It's something you build — moment by moment, decision by decision — and then protect with intention.**Legacy Goes Beyond the Balance Sheet**

Financial success is measurable.

Legacy? That's felt.

It's the way people speak about you long after you've stepped away.

It's the team you leave behind — still inspired, still empowered.

It's the values that continue to guide decisions even when your name's no longer on the door.

Legacy isn't something you claim.

It's something you leave.

And if you want it to last, you need to design your exit around it — not leave it to chance.

🔷 **Action Step:** Finish this sentence: "I want to be remembered for..."

Write it. Keep it visible. Let it shape every decision you make from here.**Operational Independence = Legacy Protection**

Here's the uncomfortable truth: if the business can't run without you, your legacy's at risk.

When everything flows through you — decisions, relationships, direction — your absence becomes a liability.

Legacy isn't about being needed forever.

It's about building something that thrives without you.

That means:

- Letting go of control
- Empowering others to lead
- Documenting your systems and values
- Creating a structure that stands, even when you're not in the room

⟐ **Action Step:** Choose one area where you're still the linchpin. Begin transitioning it to someone else, with trust and support.**Culture Needs a Succession Plan Too**

Most succession plans focus on roles and responsibilities.

But what about values and culture?

If you care about what the business feels like — not just how it operates — then your exit must include a cultural handover.

Ask yourself:

- Who understands the heart of this business?
- Who leads in a way that reflects our core values?
- How can I make sure that spirit continues?

Culture drifts when there's no compass.

Your job is to leave a clear one behind.

⟐ **Action Step:** Start a short "Leadership Legacy" memo — a simple document sharing your vision, values, and expectations for the future. It's not for legal use — it's for hearts and minds.**Start Early — Not When It's Urgent**

Legacy needs space to breathe.

If you wait until you're exhausted or cornered, you'll make rushed decisions. And rushed decisions rarely honour legacy.

Planning early gives you time to:

- Strengthen the team
- Cement your culture
- Shape the transition
- Align financials with personal values

This isn't about exiting tomorrow.

It's about being ready when the moment arrives.

◈ **Action Step:** Choose a "transition target date" — even if it's 2–3 years away. Work backwards. What needs to happen in the next 6–12 months to move toward it?**Anchor Yourself with Non-Negotiables**

There will be moments where you're tempted to bend — for speed, for money, for convenience.

But legacy is protected in the decisions you don't compromise on.

Maybe it's looking after your team.

Maybe it's only selling to someone who shares your values.

Maybe it's walking away only when the culture is secure.

Whatever it is — define it now.

◈ **Action Step:** Write down your 3 non-negotiables. Keep them at the centre of your exit process.**Leave Like You Led**

You've built something with heart.

So exit with the same level of care and clarity you used to build it.

Legacy isn't about ego.

It's not about being remembered as the hero.

It's about knowing you left behind something that still matters — something that keeps moving forward, even after you've stepped away.

Because in the end, legacy isn't the applause at the end of the journey.

It's the echo of your leadership — still ringing through the halls long after you've gone.

And that's a story worth writing well.

"You don't control what people say when you're gone — but you do shape what they remember. And that's the power of planning."

CHAPTER 3: How Much Is Enough? Valuation and Your Freedom Number

Valuation Truths: What Really Drives Your Number

"Before you chase a number, ask yourself: what are you solving for?"

Let's be real.

Business valuation is one of the most misunderstood — and most emotionally charged — parts of exit planning.

Owners hear all kinds of numbers tossed around:

"4x revenue."

"10x profit."

"A mate down the road got £3 million for his, so I should too."

But here's the uncomfortable truth:

Valuation isn't a formula.

It's a narrative. A story. A confidence game.

And the value you walk away with won't come from a spreadsheet alone. It'll come from what your business represents to the buyer — and how clearly you can show it.

Your Freedom Number Comes First

Before we dive into multiples and methods, pause for a moment.

The most important number in your exit is not what the market thinks your business is worth.

It's **how much you need** to walk away with peace of mind.

That's your **Personal Freedom Number** — the amount that lets you live life on your terms post-exit.

Whether it's £800K or £3 million — knowing your number gives you clarity. You stop chasing ego-driven goals, and start focusing on deals that actually align with your life.

◈ **Ask yourself:** If I sold today and cleared £X, would I feel free?

Profit Isn't Value — Not on Its Own

You can run a profitable business and still struggle to sell.

Why? Because buyers don't just buy profit. They buy **predictability**.

Here's the difference:

PROFIT	VALUE
Looks at the past	Looks at the future
Shows what you made	Shows what a buyer might make
Can include owner quirks	Needs normalising and adjusting

That's why **normalised EBITDA** matters.

It strips out your personal costs, inflated salaries, or once-off quirks — and tells a clean, buyer-friendly story about real earning power.

The Valuation Gap Is Real

Most deals fall apart for one simple reason: the owner wants more than the buyer is willing to pay.

This is called the **valuation gap** — and it's usually not because the buyer's cheap.

It's because:

- The business is too dependent on the owner
- There's no leadership team in place
- Revenue is lumpy or client concentration is high
- The financials are messy or unclear
- The story hasn't been packaged in a way that shows future growth

Buyers want **certainty and upside**. If they don't see it — or if you can't show it — the value drops.

Multiples Are Just a Starting Point

Yes, multiples matter. But they're not rules — they're guidelines.

A business might be worth **3x EBITDA** in one sector and **6x** in another, depending on:

- Sector dynamics
- Market appetite
- Buyer type (strategic, financial, trade, successor)
- Business resilience and transferability
- Growth potential and systems

⚠ Ignore any advisor who promises a fixed multiple before deeply reviewing your business.

Positioning Impacts Price

Two businesses with identical numbers can sell for very different amounts.

Why?

Because one **tells a better story**.

One shows future growth.

One has clear systems.

One has a strong second-tier team.

One demonstrates resilience.

One makes the buyer feel confident, not cautious.

◈ Value is as much about how the business is packaged and positioned as it is about raw profit.

Valuation Isn't a Formula — It's a Narrative

A good advisor won't just crunch numbers. They'll help you:

- Clean and normalise your financials
- Build a future-facing narrative that shows potential
- Identify and close value gaps
- Match you with the right type of buyer
- Prepare for the questions and red flags that lower price

This is why preparation matters. Most "valuation regrets" come not from the final number — but from realising too late that the business could have been worth more with better planning.

The Sooner You Start, the More You Can Shape

Valuation isn't fixed. You can influence it — over 6, 12, or 24 months — by improving:

- Your systems and reporting
- Your team's independence
- Your recurring revenue
- Your buyer positioning

It's like tending a garden. You don't force growth the night before harvest.

You water it, shape it, and get rid of the weeds early.

◈ Start shaping your valuation at least 12–18 months before exit. It's the single best way to increase what you walk away with.

The 4-Layer Valuation Check

- ◈ Personal Freedom Number
- ◈ Business Fundamentals (profit, systems, team)
- ◈ Market Trends + Sector Multiples
- ◈ Buyer-Specific Value Drivers

Final Thought: Clarity > Guesswork

Forget hearsay. Forget ego-driven benchmarks. Forget "a friend said his is worth..."

Instead, focus on three things:

◈ What's enough for your life

◈ What's realistically achievable given your business model

◈ What's worth fixing now to close the gap

Because the truth is simple:

When you understand the real levers of valuation, you stop chasing unicorns.

You start building something valuable, sellable — and most importantly, aligned with the life you want after exit.

What Buyers Really Value (And Why Profit Isn't Enough)

Let's clear something up right away:

Profit is not the same as value.

You can have strong net profits on paper... and still struggle to command a premium price.

On the flip side, a business with modest profits but strong fundamentals can attract serious buyers and strong offers.

Why?

Because buyers aren't just buying past performance — they're buying future potential.

They're not looking for your best year ever. They're looking for what's repeatable, predictable, and transferable without you.

That's where true value lives.

Normalised EBITDA: The Real Benchmark

If you've ever heard the term "EBITDA multiple," here's what it really means:

Earnings Before Interest, Tax, Depreciation, and Amortisation — adjusted to reflect the true earning power of the business.

But here's the key:

We don't use raw EBITDA. We use **normalised EBITDA** — a cleaner, truer version of your earnings that strips out one-offs, personal expenses, and anomalies.

Why? Because buyers want to see what the business will likely earn in their hands — not yours.

Examples of normalisations:

- Owner's salary adjusted to market rate
- One-off legal fees removed
- Personal car lease expenses excluded
- Notional rent added if you own the property personally

These adjustments aren't tricks — they're transparency.

They create a fair, buyer-ready picture of your real earnings.

EBITDA x Multiple = Enterprise Value (But That's Just the Start)

Once EBITDA is normalised, most buyers will use a **valuation multiple** to calculate your Enterprise Value — the starting point for negotiations.

Normalised EBITDA x Sector Multiple = Enterprise Value

Let's say your normalised EBITDA is £400,000 and your sector commands a 4x multiple.

That gives you an enterprise value of **£1.6 million**.

But don't stop there.

Buyers will adjust that number based on:

- Working capital needs
- Debt and surplus cash
- Asset values
- Business risk factors
- Growth potential
- Dependency on the owner (you)

So that £1.6M? It's a reference point — not a cheque.

Profit vs. Value: Why the Difference Matters

Here's a mistake I see all the time:

Owners assume their annual net profit is the number buyers care most about.

But here's what really drives value:

◈ Recurring revenue

◈ Strong systems and documentation

◈ A capable leadership team

◈ Diversified customer base

◈ Low customer churn

◈ Predictable cash flow

◈ Owner independence

◈ Clean, transparent financials

If your profit is high but built on shaky ground — one customer, one product, or your own hustle — the perceived risk increases, and the value drops.

But if your profit is moderate and your business is resilient, scalable, and well-structured? You might command a higher multiple than you expect.

◈ Action Step:

Start tracking your normalised EBITDA annually.

Clean up your books. Adjust for non-operating costs. And review where risk — not profit — could be dragging down value.

This gives you leverage when talking to buyers.

You're not just showing "what you made." You're showing the real, sustainable earnings the buyer can count on.

"Valuation is less about past performance — and more about future confidence."

Final Thought: Sell a Machine, Not a Moment

Buyers don't want to buy you.

They want to buy a machine that works without you — one that generates stable earnings year after year.

That's what makes a business valuable.

So yes, get your profits up.

But even more importantly — make sure those profits are systemised, transferable, and de-risked.

Because when it comes to selling a business, the how behind the numbers matters more than the numbers themselves.

From Chaos to Clarity in 8 Weeks

A few months ago, I sat down with the owners of a well-established manufacturing firm. Solid business, decent margins, loyal customer base. On the surface, it looked fine.

But once we scratched below the surface, the cracks showed.

- No succession plan
- Patchy, outdated financials
- Disengaged management team just going through the motions
- And no clear idea of how to even begin preparing for exit

In their own words, things felt "messy." They knew they wanted to sell — eventually — but didn't think anyone would take them seriously in their current state.

Sound familiar?

This is more common than you'd think. And the good news? It's fixable. In this case, it only took **eight weeks** to move from chaos to clarity — not because we rushed, but because we focused.

Here's what we did.**Step 1: The Exit Readiness Audit**

We started with a full **Exit Readiness Audit** — a structured deep dive into the business across five key areas:

- Financial performance and reporting

- Operational systems and documentation
- Leadership and succession
- Customer and supplier concentration
- Owner reliance and strategic direction

It wasn't about finding fault. It was about finding **focus** — identifying what was blocking the business from being buyer-ready.

The takeaway?

You can't fix what you haven't clearly diagnosed.

◈ **Action Step**: Run an honest, structured audit of your business. Where are you strong? Where are you vulnerable? What would a buyer see that you've been avoiding?**Step 2: Assigning Key Roles for Succession**

Next, we tackled succession — not by trying to solve everything overnight, but by starting small.

We identified the key functions still sitting solely with the owner — pricing decisions, supplier negotiations, certain client relationships — and began assigning them to senior team members.

The act of **naming roles and assigning responsibility** did two things:

1. It immediately boosted team engagement — they felt included, not excluded from the future.
2. It started reducing the buyer risk profile — a major plus when you want to increase value.

The real shift came from giving people ownership, not just tasks.

◈ **Action Step**: Identify three roles or responsibilities you're still holding onto. Assign one to a team member this week. Build a plan for the others.**Step 3: Normalising the Financials**

Their accounts had gaps. Adjustments hadn't been clearly documented. One-off costs and owner perks were baked into the profit line. It wasn't hiding anything — it just wasn't helpful for buyers.

So we walked through a **normalised EBITDA exercise** — cleaning the numbers, flagging one-off items, and presenting a clearer picture of earnings potential.

This step alone boosted their confidence massively.

They could finally see what the business was truly worth — not just what the accountant said it had made last year.

◈ **Action Step**: Review the last two years' P&Ls. Highlight any owner-related, non-recurring, or irregular costs. This is the starting point for normalisation.**Step 4: Creating the Exit Roadmap**

With clarity on where they stood, we built a clear **Exit Roadmap**:

- Timeline for handover
- Areas to de-risk
- Financial clean-up plan
- Internal communications strategy
- Key metrics to track over the next 6–12 months

No fluff. Just a simple, focused plan that gave them something they hadn't had in a while — **confidence**.

That's the power of a good roadmap. It replaces stress with structure.

◈ **Action Step**: Map out the next 90 days. What 3–5 actions would make the business more attractive to a buyer? Start there.**Final Result: A Confident, Credible Business**

Eight weeks later, this manufacturing firm was in a completely different place.

- They had a clear plan
- Key leadership roles were reassigned
- Financials were credible
- And most importantly — they felt ready to start speaking to buyers

The business hadn't changed overnight. But their positioning had.

And in the world of exits, that's everything.

The 8-Week Exit Clarity Sprint

Week 1: Personal clarity — define your freedom number
Week 2: Map current valuation and potential gaps
Week 3: Review owner dependencies
Week 4: Clean your financials
Week 5: Assess team and leadership strength
Week 6: Identify key buyer types
Week 7: Create your "exit story" narrative
Week 8: Build your pre-exit checklist

Final Thought: Clarity Is a Choice

You don't need a perfect business to begin preparing for exit.

You need:

- A clear understanding of where you are
- A commitment to address the gaps
- And a structured, focused plan to move forward

Because with the right support, even the messiest business can move from chaos to clarity — and it doesn't have to take years.

Sometimes, it just takes 8 weeks.

According to the Exit Planning Institute's 2019 report, two stats jump off the page:

- **80% of business owners don't know the value of their company**

- **75% regret their exit within 12 months**

Those numbers are staggering. And they tell us something important:

Most owners are walking into one of the biggest financial and emotional decisions of their life… unprepared.

No valuation. No roadmap. No alignment between personal goals and business realities.

And when the deal is done and the dust settles, regret sets in.

But it doesn't have to be that way. Let's break down why it happens — and more importantly, how to avoid becoming one of those 75%.**1. Know What Your Business Is Actually Worth**

Let's start with the 80%.

Most business owners simply don't know what their business is worth. They've never had a proper, independent valuation. Instead, they rely on hearsay, gut feel, or what a friend sold for a few years ago.

But valuation isn't a guessing game. And it's not just about "top line" or EBITDA — it's about:

- Transferable value

- Market appetite

- Risk profile

- Operational independence
- Recurring revenue
- Buyer perception

Without understanding the true value, everything that follows — planning, negotiation, even timing — becomes reactive.

◈ **Action Step**: Commission a valuation now, even if you're years from selling. It gives you a baseline — and reveals what's helping (or hurting) your number.**2. Don't Just Prepare the Business — Prepare Yourself**

The 75% figure around post-exit regret isn't about money.

It's about emotional readiness.

Most owners spend years — decades — pouring themselves into the business. Their identity, their time, their relationships... all wrapped up in being "the one in charge."

So when they exit — even if the deal goes well — the emotional fallout can be huge:

- Who am I without this business?
- What do I do now?
- Did I really leave on my terms?

The regret doesn't come from the transaction. It comes from the transition.

That's why emotional preparation matters just as much as financial prep.

◈ **Action Step**: Start visualising life after the exit. Journal it. Talk it through. What do your days look like? What gives you purpose? This isn't fluff — it's foundational.**3. Align Your Exit Strategy with Your Life Goals**

One of the biggest causes of regret is misalignment.

An owner sells, but later realises the exit didn't reflect what actually mattered most.

Maybe they compromised on culture.

Maybe they took the wrong deal because the number was high.

Maybe they stayed too long — or left too fast.

The solution? **Get clear on what you want.** Personally and professionally.

Your exit isn't just a business event. It's a life chapter.

• Do you want full retirement or phased involvement?

• Do you want to sell to a strategic buyer or someone who'll keep your legacy alive?

• Do you need a clean break, or time to gradually step out?

◈ **Action Step**: Define your "exit principles" — 3–5 non-negotiables that align with your values, goals, and lifestyle. Use them as filters for every future decision.**4. Set Up Systems That Let the Business Run Without You**

Here's another regret trap: owners who want to sell... but can't.

Because the business is too dependent on them.

- They approve every quote
- They hold key customer relationships
- They're the centre of the wheel

And when they're gone, the buyer sees risk — and that risk kills value.

The fix? Start building operational independence now.

The more the business runs without you, the more valuable and sellable it becomes.

◈ **Action Step**: Pick one task you still own that someone else should manage. Delegate it this month — and document the process while you're at it.**Final Thought: Exit with Clarity, Not Regret**

These stats from the Exit Planning Institute are a wake-up call — not a warning sign.

Most regret comes from not preparing — not knowing what the business is worth, not planning for life after, not being clear on what really matters.

But with the right approach, your exit can be something else entirely:

- Empowering
- Fulfilling
- Aligned

- And maybe even enjoyable

Start early. Get the facts. Prepare yourself.

Because when you exit with clarity, you don't just close a chapter.

You start the next one with confidence.

"Regret happens when exits are rushed, reactive, or misaligned with the owner's truth. Clarity is the antidote."

CHAPTER 4: Building Independence — Reducing Owner Reliance

How to Make Your Business Less Dependent on You

"If you're the engine, the steering wheel, and the seatbelt — your business can't be sold. It can only be handed back."

One of the biggest barriers to a successful exit — or even just taking a proper holiday — is a business that depends too heavily on the owner.

If everything runs through you, if your team can't make decisions without checking in, if the business feels like a house of cards when you're away — you're not running a company, you're holding up a system.

And buyers? They see that.

They don't just ask what's the EBITDA?

They ask what happens when you're not here?

So if you're thinking about exiting (or just want to free yourself from the day-to-day), one of the smartest moves you can make is this:

Build a business that doesn't need you.

Let's walk through how to actually do that.

Where Are You Still the Bottleneck?

- Sales approvals?
- Strategic decisions?
- Client retention?
- Operations?

1. Build Clear, Documented Systems

If your business runs on unwritten rules and mental checklists, you're not alone — but it's time to change that.

Start documenting:

- How clients are onboarded
- How quotes are created
- What happens when a new hire joins
- The way customer issues are handled
- Weekly, monthly, quarterly routines

This creates consistency, scalability, and independence.

Anyone can step in and follow a process — no mind-reading required.

◈ **Action Step**: Choose one recurring task you handle personally. Write down the steps, turn it into a checklist, and train someone else to own it.**2. Empower a Capable Management Team**

A strong second layer of leadership is one of the biggest value drivers in any business.

You don't need a full corporate org chart — just a few key people who:

- Take ownership of outcomes
- Are empowered to make decisions
- Understand the vision and values
- Can keep things moving in your absence

You can't exit — or even scale — if you're the single point of failure.

🧭 **Action Step**: Identify your top 2–3 future leaders. Meet with them regularly, share context, and give them space to grow into their roles.**3. Delegate Decision-Making — For Real**

This one's tough. You might trust your team... but still jump in when things get uncertain.

The problem? If your team senses you'll always step in, they'll stop stepping up.

Start shifting the dynamic:

- Ask your team to present options, not just problems
- Define clear decision boundaries (what they can own vs. what needs escalation)
- Back them — even when they make small mistakes

True delegation isn't about giving people tasks. It's about giving them authority.

🧭 **Action Step**: Choose one decision you normally make. Hand it over — and don't take it back.**4. Centralise Knowledge**

When knowledge lives in your head (or scattered across inboxes and notebooks), it's a liability.

Instead, build a shared, living resource — a digital playbook, an operations manual, even a shared drive with key info.

Think:

- How-to guides

- Templates and forms
- Key contacts
- Training videos
- FAQs and decision trees

This reduces your team's dependence on you and increases the speed and consistency of how things get done.

◈ **Action Step**: Start a shared folder titled "How We Do Things." Upload one helpful document each week.**5. Leverage Automation and Tech**

If you're still doing routine tasks manually — chasing invoices, replying to repeat enquiries, juggling spreadsheets — there's probably a smarter way.

Use technology to:

- Automate recurring admin
- Standardise communication
- Track metrics and performance
- Streamline onboarding

Every task you remove from your daily plate makes your business more self-sufficient — and more appealing to a buyer.

◈ **Action Step**: Identify one task you do regularly that software could automate. Research and implement a simple solution within 30 days.**6. Step Back (Strategically)**

The best way to test whether your business can run without you... is to actually step back.

Take a week off and watch what happens.

Reduce your hours and observe the gaps.

Stop checking every detail and see who steps up.

This isn't about neglect — it's about resilience. It shows you what's working — and where you still need to develop people, systems, or structure.

◈ **Action Step**: Book a week off in the next three months — and don't take your laptop.**Final Thought: Your Role Should Evolve, Not Disappear**

You don't have to vanish overnight.

But your role should shift from "doing everything" to "steering the ship."

When your business can thrive without you, you're no longer trapped — you're free.

Free to exit, to grow, to slow down, or just to choose your next chapter.

And that's when your business becomes not just valuable...

But truly independent.

The Key People Question: Who Stays, Who Goes, Who Leads

When it comes to preparing for an exit, most owners spend a lot of time on financials, systems, and valuation.

But there's another critical piece that often gets pushed to the side — and yet, it's one of the biggest drivers of value in any deal:

Your people.

Buyers don't just invest in numbers. They invest in continuity — in the team who'll carry the business forward. So one of the most important (and sometimes uncomfortable) questions you'll face is this:

Who stays? Who goes? And who leads when you step back?

Let's break that down in a way that's practical — and doable.

"Imagine a buyer asking: 'Who do I rely on once you're gone?' — can you answer with confidence?"

1. Evaluate Roles Through a Strategic Lens

Start by reviewing your team structure. Not just who's doing what — but whether their role contributes to the future of the business.

Ask:

- Is this role still needed in the next chapter?
- Does this person align with where the business is going?

• If they left, would the business take a hit — or could someone else step up?

This isn't about being ruthless. It's about being realistic. Roles that made sense five years ago might not be right for the next phase.

◈ **Action Step**: List your top 10 roles. For each, ask: is this role future-critical, transition-critical, or legacy-only?**2. Identify Potential Leaders Early**

Don't wait until the exit is on the table to think about succession.

Look at your current team and ask:

• Who shows up consistently under pressure?

• Who earns trust — across departments or teams?

• Who demonstrates both resilience and humility?

You're looking for **character as much as capability**. Skills can be taught. Integrity can't.

And here's something important: your top performers aren't always your future leaders. High performance doesn't always equal high potential.

Leadership is about long-term mindset — not just hitting short-term targets.

◈ **Action Step**: Identify your top 2 internal leadership candidates. Book monthly 1:1s to support their growth and start gradually increasing their decision-making authority.**3. Culture Over Credentials**

In an exit scenario, buyers want to know that your culture is healthy — because culture drives performance, retention, and customer experience.

So as you assess your team, prioritise **cultural alignment.** Who lives the values? Who supports others? Who brings energy to the room?

Someone might have all the skills on paper... but if they drain morale, resist change, or clash with the rest of the team, they could create more risk than value.

⟐ **Action Step**: For each key person, score them on two things: technical contribution and cultural contribution. Use that insight to guide retention or promotion decisions.**4. Plan for Succession Before You Need It**

Succession planning isn't just about picking a name. It's about creating a **transition path** — with time to coach, support, and embed new leadership before you step away.

That means:

• Defining what success looks like in that role

• Setting expectations clearly

• Giving the person space to grow into it while you're still around

This gives buyers confidence. It gives your team stability. And it gives you breathing room to exit at your pace — not out of panic.

🔍 **Action Step**: Write down your 3 most critical roles. Who's the next in line — internally or externally? If the role is vacant, start building the succession plan now.**5. Mitigate the Risk of Losing Key People**

One of the biggest fears for buyers is that the "glue" holding the business together — often a few key people — might leave right after the sale.

To reduce this risk:

- Identify who's vital to operations, relationships, or knowledge transfer
- Understand what motivates them to stay
- Consider retention plans, bonuses, or involvement in the transition process

It's not about locking people in. It's about treating them fairly, keeping them informed, and giving them a reason to be part of the next chapter.

🔍 **Action Step**: Have a one-to-one conversation with each critical team member. Share your vision, get their input, and explore what support they need to stay engaged during the transition.**Final Thought: People Drive Value — and Continuity**

You've spent years building your business.

But the strength of your team — and your clarity about who stays, who goes, and who leads — will shape what it's worth, and how smoothly the exit plays out.

Start early. Be honest. Support your people with care and structure.

Because when your business is ready to run without you — led by the right people, in the right roles — that's not just exit readiness.

That's leadership legacy.

"Systems aren't just for buyers. They give you freedom now."

Creating Systems Buyers Love (And You'll Never Regret)

One of the biggest turning points in any exit journey is this realisation:

"The more your business depends on systems, not you, the more valuable it becomes."

Buyers don't just want a successful business.

They want a business that's repeatable, scalable, and transferable.

And nothing signals that louder than well-designed systems.

But here's the secret sauce: these aren't just systems buyers love — they're systems you'll never regret building, because they also make your business easier to run, easier to grow, and far less stressful to manage.

Let's explore how to build those systems — and where to focus first.**1. Start with What Buyers Actually Want**

Buyers aren't just interested in what you do — they're interested in how you do it.

They're asking:

- "Is this business efficient?"
- "Can it scale?"
- "Does it run without the owner holding everything together?"

Your job is to show them "yes" with confidence — through your systems.

So where should you focus?

◈ **Action Step**: Identify your business's top 3 value drivers (e.g., lead generation, customer retention, fulfilment). Build systems that lock in consistency around each one.**2. Systemise What Makes You Special**

Every business has a few areas where it quietly excels — the things that keep customers coming back or give you a unique edge.

Maybe it's how you onboard clients.

Maybe it's your customer service workflow.

Maybe it's your team's ability to deliver fast, without quality slipping.

Systemise that.

When you document, refine, and embed those strengths into clear processes, they become assets — not just habits. That makes them transferable to a new owner, and scalable beyond your own effort.

◈ **Action Step**: Choose one internal strength that gives you an edge. Create a simple SOP (standard operating procedure) or checklist that captures it.**3. Build for Sustainability, Not Just Sale**

Great systems aren't just about impressing buyers — they make your life better, too.

You reduce firefighting.

Your team becomes more accountable.

Things don't grind to a halt when you take a day off.

And when it's time to exit, you're not scrambling to explain how everything works — it's already there in black and white.

◈ **Action Step**: Audit one part of your business this month (e.g., sales, delivery, admin). Where are the inefficiencies or bottlenecks? Start fixing those first — it'll benefit you now and add value later.**4. Financial Systems = Confidence**

Let's be honest — many owners delay this part.

Invoices in one folder, receipts in another. A spreadsheet here, a notebook there.

But to a buyer, clarity equals confidence.

Your financial systems should show:

- Consistent reporting
- Clean records (ideally monthly management accounts)
- Adjustments clearly labelled (owner perks, one-offs, etc.)
- The true earning potential of the business

This is where deals are made or lost.

◈ **Action Step**: Set up monthly financial reporting (if you don't already). Meet with your accountant or bookkeeper to review the last 12 months and begin tracking EBITDA and normalised profit consistently.**5. Independence = Transferable Value**

Buyers want a business that can run without you.

So your systems must support that independence — not fight against it.

That means:

- Documented operations
- Clear KPIs and dashboards
- Defined roles and responsibilities
- Decision-making protocols
- Technology that supports, not complicates

If you had to step out for 90 days, would the business keep running? That's the ultimate systems test.

◈ **Action Step**: Create a "handover-ready" playbook. One place where all critical systems, contacts, tools, and SOPs are stored — and accessible to your leadership team.**Final Thought: Systemise Your Way to Freedom and Value**

Systems are more than admin.

They're the **invisible engine** that makes your business repeatable, scalable, and sellable.

They reduce risk.

They increase buyer confidence.

And they give you peace of mind — whether you're planning an exit or simply want more freedom now.

So build systems not just to "get out" one day...

But to run better today, and scale smarter tomorrow.

Because when your business runs on systems — not you — you're building something truly valuable.

If there's one book I believe every business owner should read before even thinking about an exit, it's **Built to Sell** by John Warrillow.

It's not a dense manual or a technical finance guide. It's a story — but one that hits home for thousands of founders. Because the message is simple, powerful, and unavoidable:

If your business can't run without you, it's not sellable.

Warrillow doesn't just point out the problem. He shows what it looks like to transform a business from owner-dependent to owner-independent — and why that shift makes all the difference when it comes to value, scalability, and peace of mind.

Let's unpack the big ideas — and how to apply them to your own business.**1. Stop Being the Business**

Most owners build something that works — but only because they're in it, every day, holding it together.

Sales? You.

Client relationships? You.

Operations, pricing, problem-solving, decisions? You again.

It works... until it doesn't. And when you try to step back, the business wobbles — or worse, stops.

That's the first wake-up call in Built to Sell:

You need to build a business that can thrive without you.

Buyers aren't buying you. They're buying what remains when you are gone.

◈ **Action Step**: Write down 5 things only you currently do. Then choose one to delegate this month — and document the process as you go.**2. Specialise to Scale**

One of the core messages in the book is to focus on a **scalable, repeatable offering**.

The story's main character runs a creative agency doing custom work for every client. Sound familiar? It's how many service businesses operate — saying yes to everything, solving different problems each time.

But buyers want predictability. They want systems, not chaos.

So the owner picks one service — logo design — and builds a process that's streamlined, repeatable, and easy to train.

And guess what? The business becomes more valuable, more efficient, and easier to sell.

◈ **Action Step**: What's one offering in your business you could standardise or productise? Focus on building repeatable delivery around it.**3. Systemise and Simplify**

Warrillow hammers home the power of **documented systems**. Why? Because systems reduce reliance on people (especially you) and allow others to deliver with consistency.

Think onboarding, quoting, service delivery, follow-up — every repeatable task should have a playbook.

Not only does this improve efficiency, but it also builds **buyer confidence**. A buyer sees a business with systems and thinks: I can step into this without chaos.

◈ **Action Step**: Choose one area of your business (e.g. sales, delivery, admin). Create a simple SOP or checklist for how it's done. Share it with your team.**4. Build a Team That Can Run the Business**

The owner in Built to Sell learns to **hire and trust** capable people. He moves from doing everything to leading a team.

You don't need a corporate structure. But you do need a few key people who:

- Know the systems
- Take responsibility
- Can make decisions without you

Buyers love this. It reduces key-person risk and shows the business can run long after you've left.

◈ **Action Step**: Identify your top two potential successors. Start mentoring them. Give them ownership over an area of the business.**5. Make Yourself Replaceable — and Valuable**

It's ironic. The more you remove yourself from day-to-day operations, the more valuable your business becomes.

You stop being the bottleneck.

Your time becomes more strategic.

And your business starts to look like an asset, not a job.

That's what buyers want. And that's what Built to Sell teaches so well:

A saleable business is one that works — with or without you.**Final Thought: Don't Just Read It** — Live **It**

Built to Sell isn't just a book. It's a blueprint.

It gives you permission to stop being the superhero — and start building a system.

It helps you reframe what value really means.

It challenges you to simplify, systemise, and step back.

So if you haven't read it yet, pick it up.

And if you have? Pick it up again.

Because building a business that can be sold isn't just about exit.

It's about freedom — today and tomorrow.

If you've ever found yourself thinking, "We've got the skills, so why do things still feel stuck?" — you're not alone.

In fact, that's exactly what Patrick Lencioni's book **The Five Dysfunctions of a Team** unpacks. And if you're preparing for an exit — or even just trying to build a business that doesn't revolve around you — this model becomes incredibly relevant.

Because here's the truth: your team's culture, trust levels, and leadership dynamics will either support your exit... or quietly derail it.

Let's break it down in plain English — with practical takeaways you can use right now.**1. Absence of Trust: The Silent Killer**

This isn't about trusting someone to do their job — it's about **vulnerability-based trust**.

Can your team admit mistakes? Say "I don't know"? Ask for help without fear?

When trust is missing, people stay guarded. They play it safe. And progress slows.

◈ **Action Step**: Lead with vulnerability. Share a past mistake in a team meeting. Invite others to reflect on lessons learned. It sets the tone for openness.**2. Fear of Conflict: The Fake Harmony Trap**

When trust is low, people avoid healthy disagreement. Everything feels polite on the surface, but underneath, there's frustration, tension, and a lack of clarity.

The absence of open conflict doesn't mean alignment — it means avoidance.

Healthy teams **debate issues, not each other**. They push back, speak up, and challenge ideas — because they care about getting it right, not being right.

◈ **Action Step**: In your next team session, ask: "What's one decision we've made recently that deserves more debate?" Model constructive challenge — and praise those who speak up.**3. Lack of Commitment: Death by Maybe**

If people don't speak up during decisions, they don't commit to the outcome.

They nod, smile, and quietly disengage. Which means follow-through drops, and accountability becomes impossible.

Clarity and buy-in go hand in hand — and both are needed for progress.

◈ **Action Step**: End key meetings with a summary: "Here's what we've agreed, and who owns it." Confirm alignment out loud — and let silence mean "no" instead of "yes."**4. Avoidance of Accountability: No Ownership, No Progress**

When there's no commitment, accountability falls through the cracks.

People hesitate to call out underperformance. Leaders overfunction to compensate. And mediocrity becomes normal.

High-performing teams **hold each other accountable — sideways, not just top-down**.

◈ **Action Step**: Introduce a shared scoreboard. Make team commitments visible, time-bound, and owned. Review them publicly in meetings. Peer accountability raises the bar.**5. Inattention to Results: When Egos Get in the Way**

The final dysfunction shows up when team members prioritise **individual success over collective goals**.

Departments compete. Leaders protect turf. Progress stalls.

A transition-ready team is united around shared outcomes — whether that's growth, exit readiness, or operational independence.

🔶 **Action Step**: Define 1–3 key collective results that matter right now (e.g. revenue growth, systemisation, reducing owner reliance). Link team actions directly to those outcomes in weekly reviews.**Why This Matters So Much in Exit Planning**

If you're planning to exit, your business needs to function without you.

That means:

- A leadership team that trusts each other
- A culture of healthy debate
- Aligned goals
- Accountability without babysitting
- Focused execution on what matters most

Without that? You end up stuck in the middle — too involved, too frustrated, and too dependent on your own presence to ever step away.

Fixing the five dysfunctions doesn't happen overnight — but the shift starts with awareness and small actions.

You don't need to be perfect. You just need to be committed to building a team that operates with trust, alignment, and accountability.

Because that's what buyers want.

And more importantly, it's what frees you up — for exit, for growth, or just for a life that doesn't revolve around the next internal fire.

When Stephen Covey said, "Begin with the end in mind," he wasn't just offering a productivity hack — he was planting a foundational truth.

For business owners, that one habit might be the difference between a rewarding, strategic exit and a last-minute scramble filled with regret.

Most owners start their business with survival in mind. Then growth. Then maybe freedom.

Very few start with the **exit** in mind — let alone legacy, transition, or long-term value creation.

But here's what I've learned (and what Covey so clearly understood):

You don't build a sellable business by accident.

You design it that way — on purpose — from the very start.

Let's break this down.**Envision Your Exit — Not as the End, but as a Goal**

When you picture your exit, what do you see?

Is it a sale to a strategic buyer?

A management buyout?

A family transition?

Or maybe just stepping away while the business continues to thrive without you?

Whatever your vision, defining it early gives your business direction. It helps you make smarter decisions — about people, systems, investment, and even your role — that align with your bigger picture.

◈ **Action Step**: Take 10 minutes this week to write down your ideal exit scenario. Include not just the financial outcome, but also how you want the business to continue and how you want to feel at the end.**Design a Business That Can Outlast You**

This is where Covey's principle really takes shape.

If the end goal is a business that survives and thrives without you, you need to:

- Document and delegate
- Develop leaders
- Systemise key operations
- Remove bottlenecks
- Build resilience

In short, you stop being the business and start building a business — one that others can run, buy, or inherit without fear of collapse.

◈ **Action Step**: Choose one key function (sales, delivery, operations) and begin documenting how it works. Aim to hand it off within 3–6 months.**Set Milestones That Keep You on Track**

It's easy to drift in the day-to-day, especially when things are "working well enough."

But when you begin with the end in mind, you can work backwards to create clear milestones — and those checkpoints keep you honest.

- When should your systems be fully documented?
- When should your top team be in place?

• When will you run your first valuation check?

A long-term goal needs short-term actions.

◈ **Action Step**: Set three 90-day goals that move you closer to a business that could run — or be sold — without you. Track them weekly.**Evaluate Your Business Like a Buyer Would**

If you're serious about one day stepping away, you need to look at your business the way a buyer would.

Ask:

• Is the revenue repeatable?

• Are the earnings sustainable?

• Is the team capable?

• Are the risks manageable?

You don't need to be perfect. But you do need to see the gaps — and take action over time to close them.

◈ **Action Step**: Run a "buyer's lens" audit. Rate your business from 1–5 across profitability, systems, team strength, and owner reliance. Use the lowest score as your next priority.**Build for Value — Not Just Income**

A business that delivers a great salary but zero transferable value is a job, not an asset.

When you build with the end in mind, you shift your focus:

- From short-term income to long-term equity
- From your name to the brand
- From daily grind to strategic design

That shift doesn't just benefit your future buyer — it benefits you, now.

It gives you more freedom, more options, and more peace of mind.**Final Thought: Build the Business You'd Want to Buy**

If you were buying your own business tomorrow, what would you want to see?

Clear systems? A strong team? Solid profits? Low dependency on the founder?

That's the business you need to build.

And it starts now — by getting clear on where you're headed.

Stephen Covey had it right.

When you begin with the end in mind, you don't just build a better business.

You build a future you'll actually enjoy living in.

Peter Drucker famously said,

"The greatest danger in times of turbulence is not the turbulence — it is to act with yesterday's logic."

And let's be honest — we've all done it.

We stick to what used to work.

We cling to old playbooks.

We double down on familiarity, even when the ground beneath us is shifting.

But here's the hard truth: turbulence doesn't wait for us to catch up.

Whether you're navigating economic shocks, market disruption, changing buyer behaviour, or even preparing for a business exit — **your ability to adapt matters more than your ability to predict.Yesterday's Logic Feels Safe — Until It Isn't**

Most businesses are built on habits.

"We've always done it this way."

"That's how we've served clients for years."

"Our model works — why change it?"

But in times of turbulence — and let's face it, we're in one of those times right now — old logic becomes a liability.

Yesterday's logic might've brought you here, but it won't carry you forward. The market evolves. Buyers evolve. Your business has to as well.

◈ **Action Step**: Identify one process, product, or mindset in your business that hasn't changed in 3+ years. Ask: "Is this still relevant today — or just familiar?"**The New Competitive Edge: Adaptability**

If there's one thing that gives you an edge in a volatile world, it's **adaptive thinking**.

That means:

- Staying curious
- Challenging assumptions
- Testing new ideas quickly
- Letting go of what no longer serves the business

And it's not just about surviving — it's about unlocking opportunities you wouldn't have seen while clinging to the old way of doing things.

Think of it like pruning a tree: letting go isn't loss — it's preparation for healthier growth.

◈ **Action Step**: Hold a team session titled "What Should We Let Go Of?" Invite input. Explore ideas. Create space for innovation.**Innovation Isn't Just for the Big Players**

You don't need to be a tech giant to innovate.

Innovation in a small business might look like:

- Streamlining client onboarding
- Automating follow-ups
- Switching to subscription pricing

- Outsourcing non-core tasks
- Repositioning services for new market needs

These aren't moonshots. They're practical evolutions that make your business leaner, smarter, and more appealing — especially to buyers looking for modern, resilient operations.

◈ **Action Step**: Choose one small area of the business and ask, "How could this be done 50% better or faster?" Test a simple change this month.**Empower Your Team to Think Differently**

One person — especially the owner — can't carry the entire weight of change. Your team must feel safe, supported, and equipped to think differently, act quickly, and learn as they go.

That means:

- Encouraging experimentation
- Celebrating lessons, not just wins
- Providing tools and feedback loops
- Leading by example

When the culture supports adaptation, progress becomes normal — not just reactive.

◈ **Action Step**: Start a monthly "Ideas in Action" review. Ask the team to submit small changes they've tested. Share results. Reward learning.**Exit Planning Requires Present-Moment Logic**

Here's where this becomes deeply personal.

If you're preparing for an exit — even 2 to 3 years out — acting with yesterday's logic is one of the biggest risks you'll face.

Buyers are looking for:

- Operational efficiency
- Tech-enabled processes
- Resilient teams
- Modern systems
- Scalable delivery

If your business feels outdated or owner-reliant, it will struggle to command full value — or even attract interest.

⟐ **Action Step**: Review your tech stack, systems, and structure. Are you building for yesterday's market — or tomorrow's buyer?**Final Thought: Change Isn't the Enemy — Complacency Is**

Turbulence will come and go.

Markets will shift. Technology will evolve. Buyer expectations will rise.

The danger isn't the change.

It's the mindset that says, "We're fine as we are."

So take Drucker's wisdom to heart.

Don't resist change — lead it.

Don't wait to be disrupted — reinvent before you have to.

Because the owners who succeed, grow, and exit on their terms aren't the ones with perfect plans.

They're the ones who stay flexible — and act with today's logic.

Your Exit Is Not a Transaction—It's a Transformation

There's a common myth in the business world that your exit is just a deal — a simple buy-sell event.

It's not.

If you've poured years — maybe decades — of energy, identity, and purpose into building your business, walking away isn't just a spreadsheet moment. It's a **personal, emotional, and strategic transformation.**

The truth is, you're not just selling a business. You're stepping into a new chapter of life. And how you plan for that shift makes all the difference between relief... and regret.

So let's explore how to treat your exit not as a transaction, but as a transformation — with intention, clarity, and alignment.**1. Start with** Why **You're Exiting**

Before any legal, tax, or financial prep — pause and ask yourself: Why now?

Are you tired? Ready for freedom? Want more time with family? Looking for a change of pace?

Clarity around your true motivation brings focus to every decision that follows — from choosing the right buyer, to structuring the deal, to deciding how much involvement (if any) you want post-exit.

◈ **Action Step**: Write down your top 3 personal goals post-exit. This helps anchor your decisions in purpose, not pressure.**2. Align the Exit with Your Life — Not Just Your Business**

A great exit doesn't just cash out the business. It supports your life — financially, emotionally, and practically.

That means asking:

- What lifestyle do I want after this?
- What does freedom really look like for me?
- How much is "enough" to feel secure?

Your exit plan should work backwards from your life goals — not the other way around.

◈ **Action Step**: Define your Personal Freedom Number — the amount of post-tax cash (or income stream) that gives you comfort and choice.**3. Build a Business That Can Stand Without You**

This one's crucial: the more your business relies on you, the less valuable (and sellable) it is.

Buyers don't just buy assets — they buy continuity. And continuity without you means:

- Documented systems
- A team that can lead
- Clear roles and workflows
- Strong client relationships that aren't all tied to you

◈ **Action Step**: List the top 5 things only you can do in the business. Start delegating or systemising one per quarter.**4. Know What Makes Your Business Valuable to Buyers**

Not all revenue is created equal. What buyers care about are value drivers:

- Recurring income
- Diversified customer base
- Profit margins
- Operational stability
- Brand reputation
- Scalable systems

If you want a strong exit, you need to understand — and articulate — these drivers.

◈ **Action Step**: Create a one-page summary of your business's key value drivers. Use this as the foundation for discussions with advisors or buyers.**5. Prepare Emotionally, Not Just Financially**

This is the part most owners skip — and it's why so many experience regret within a year of selling.

Exiting a business changes your identity. Your routines. Your sense of purpose.

If you haven't thought about what's next, the transition can feel hollow — even if the deal was "successful" on paper.

You need something to move toward, not just away from.

◈ **Action Step**: Begin shaping your post-exit life plan. What projects, passions, or pursuits excite you? Who do you want to become after the business?**6. Cover the Legal, Tax, and Transition Details Early**

Yes, exit is emotional. But it's also practical.

Leaving the legal and tax structuring to the last minute can cost you dearly — in both stress and real money.

Build the right team of advisors early: legal, tax, financial, and strategic. Let them help you transition on your terms, not under pressure.

◈ **Action Step**: Book an initial meeting with a tax advisor who understands business sales. Ask: "What should I be thinking about 1–2 years ahead of an exit?"**Final Thought: Exit Isn't the End — It's the Evolution**

Your exit doesn't need to be a dramatic curtain drop.

It can be a transition into something that reflects who you've become — and who you're becoming next.

So don't treat it like a transaction.

Treat it like a turning point.

Because when your exit is rooted in purpose, alignment, and legacy — it's not just about leaving.

It's about becoming.

Communicating the Exit Internally (Without Panic)

Let's be honest — telling your team you're planning to exit the business can feel like dropping a bomb.

The worry is real: Will they panic? Will they think the company's collapsing? Will key people leave before the ink's dry?

Handled poorly, internal communication around your exit can cause real disruption. But handled well? It can build trust, reinforce your leadership, and even rally your team behind the transition.

So let's talk about how to do it without panic, without drama, and in a way that protects your people, your culture, and your legacy. **1. Start with Your Core Leadership Team**

Before you make any kind of broader announcement, gather your key leaders. These are the people who'll carry the message, steady the team, and help keep the wheels turning.

Engaging them early creates buy-in and allows you to sense-check your messaging. It also shows respect — and builds the trust you'll need throughout the transition.

◈ **Action Step**: Create a short leadership meeting agenda: **2. Create a Communication Plan (Not Just a One-Off Email)**

• Why now?

• What's staying the same?

• What we know (and what we don't yet)

- How they can help lead

Your exit isn't a one-time announcement — it's a journey.

And every audience (leadership, staff, customers, suppliers) needs slightly different messaging. What's critical is clarity, consistency, and timing.

Start by thinking through:

- Who needs to know what, and when?
- What tone will you use — calm, transparent, confident?
- What are the likely concerns, and how can you address them upfront?

A good plan turns potential panic into clarity and calm.

◈ **Action Step**: Write a short FAQ for employees. Cover key questions like:**3. Be Honest — But Reassuring**

- Why are you exiting?
- What's the timeline?
- Will my job be affected?
- What happens next?

You don't need to share every detail of the sale process. But you do need to speak with transparency and empathy.

Let your team know what's happening and why. Acknowledge uncertainty — but focus on what's staying the same. Reaffirm your commitment to a smooth transition.

Panic comes from the unknown. Honesty and clarity keep it in check.

◈ **Action Step**: Draft your announcement with this structure:**4. Speak to the Human Side of the Transition**

- What's changing
- What's not
- Why this matters (for the company and the team)
- Your ongoing commitment
- What support will be available

Even if you're excited about your exit, some of your team might feel shocked, scared, or even betrayed. That's normal — and it deserves space.

Make time for Q&A. Ask how they're feeling. Offer reassurance where you can — and support where needed.

A little empathy goes a long way in maintaining morale and loyalty.

◈ **Action Step**: After your announcement, block out one-on-one time with key team members. Let them ask questions privately, voice concerns, and feel heard.**5. Reinforce the Vision — And Their Role in It**

This isn't just about your exit. It's about the company's future — and your team's place in it.

Make sure they understand:

- The vision remains
- Their contributions still matter
- The transition is designed to preserve and grow what you've built

If you can paint a compelling future beyond your departure, people will feel more grounded — and more motivated.

◈ **Action Step**: End your team announcement by restating the company's core values and long-term direction. Let them know the legacy isn't ending — it's evolving.**Final Thought: Don't Let Silence Speak for You**

In the absence of information, people make up their own stories.

So be proactive. Speak early, speak clearly, and keep speaking — even when there's "nothing new" to report.

Because your team doesn't just need updates.

They need leadership.

They need reassurance.

They need to know they're still part of something meaningful.

And when you handle internal communication with care, empathy, and structure — you don't just manage a transition.

You protect your culture.

You honour your people.

And you preserve your legacy — the right way.

"People remember how you made them feel — especially when big changes happen."

CHAPTER 5: Mastering the Financials — The Real Story Behind Value

"Buyers don't buy potential. They buy predictability — and nothing screams confidence like a clean, steady profit line."

When preparing to sell your business, one of the biggest blind spots isn't valuation. It isn't tax. It isn't even succession planning.

It's **financial clarity**.

That's where Mike Michalowicz's Profit First framework becomes surprisingly relevant — even though the book isn't about exits.

Because if you can't clearly see how profitable your business really is — or worse, you're constantly juggling cash — how can a buyer?

Profit First flips the traditional model on its head:

Instead of "Sales – Expenses = Profit," it becomes:

Sales – Profit = Expenses.

Simple. But powerful.

Because when you prioritise profit first, you change how your business thinks, spends, and grows — which is exactly what a buyer wants to see.

Let's break down what this means for exit readiness.

Blind Spot	Impact on Exit
Overstated revenue	Distrust
Mixed personal costs	Hard to normalise
No working capital plan	Reduces headline price

1. Prioritising Profit Builds Financial Stability

At its core, Profit First is about creating discipline.

You don't wait to see what's left over — you take your profit first and run the business within what remains. It forces clarity, constraint, and control.

From an exit perspective, this makes you attractive.

It shows that your business:

- Operates lean
- Manages cash effectively
- Is not reliant on debt or crisis borrowing
- Generates consistent, visible profit

◈ **Action Step**: Open a separate profit account. Start transferring a small percentage of income into it before paying expenses. Even 1% builds the habit.**2. Know Your True Profitability**

Many business owners confuse top-line revenue with success. Or they think they're "doing okay" because they have money in the account.

But buyers want visibility. They want to know:

- What's recurring?
- What's normalised EBITDA?
- What adjustments are there for owner lifestyle costs?

The Profit First mindset forces you to stop blurring the lines — and that's critical when presenting your business for sale.

◈ **Action Step**: Work with your accountant to create a **normalised profit and loss** statement — stripping out personal expenses, one-offs, and anything a buyer wouldn't inherit.**3. Simplify Decision-Making Through Structure**

Profit First isn't just about bank accounts. It's about giving every pound a purpose.

By splitting money into categories (profit, tax, owner pay, operating expenses), you simplify decisions. You know what's available — and what's not.

That clarity makes your business easier to run and easier to evaluate. No grey areas. No surprises. Just clean, intentional flow.

◈ **Action Step**: Set up 3–5 core accounts:**4. Buyers Love Financial Discipline**

- **Income** (where all revenue lands)
- **Profit** (your reward)
- **Owner's Pay** (your salary)
- **Tax** (avoid the surprise bill)
- **Opex** (what's left to run the business)

Imagine being a buyer and seeing this:

- Profit allocated monthly
- Taxes accounted for
- Clean accounts
- No frantic year-end reconciliations
- Reliable cash flow

Now compare that to:

- One big account
- Poor forecasting
- Owner perks hidden in the books
- Reactive decision-making

Which one would you pay more for?

Exactly.

◈ **Action Step**: Include a "financial operations summary" in your exit prep pack. Explain how money is managed, what systems you use, and how profit is monitored.**5. Profit Builds Confidence — For You and Your Buyer**

There's something deeply empowering about taking profit intentionally every month.

Not only does it create consistency — it builds confidence.

You stop operating on hope or momentum. You start seeing your business as an asset — one that rewards you now and positions you well for exit later.

Buyers don't just want numbers — they want confidence in the numbers. Profit First helps you provide both.

◈ **Action Step**: Review your last 6 months of financials. What would they say to a buyer? Is the profit obvious, consistent, and clean?**Final Thought: Exit-Ready Starts with Profit-Ready**

Profit First might not be an "exit book," but it's one of the most practical financial systems for any owner preparing to sell.

It forces clarity.

It builds discipline.

It simplifies the business for everyone — including you.

So whether your exit is one year or five years away, start treating profit like the non-negotiable it is.

Because when you lead with profit, you don't just build a healthier business.

You build one that's worth buying.

The Day I Knew I Had to Rebuild

There's a moment that stays burned into your memory forever. Mine happened in a car park, engine off, silence heavy — with exactly **£3.24** in my pocket.

That was it.

No safety net.

No options.

Just me, staring down the reality that everything I'd worked for had fallen apart.

Money? Gone.

Reputation? In tatters.

Relationships? Fractured, if not lost.

My sense of self? Barely intact.

And yet, in the middle of that wreckage, one thought came through louder than all the noise:

"You either rebuild, or you disappear."

That moment — not the years before or the success after — is what shaped everything I've built since.**Rock Bottom Brings Radical Clarity**

It's strange, but there's a certain stillness that comes with collapse. When you lose everything, all the noise falls away. You stop pretending. You stop performing. You see things for what they really are.

In that moment, I realised something powerful:

No one was coming to save me.

The only way forward was a choice — a real one — to stop spiralling and start rebuilding.

And that's where it begins for all of us.

Not with a bank loan.

Not with a LinkedIn post.

But with a clear, quiet decision:

"I'm not done."Rebuilding Isn't About Recovery — It's About Renewal

Most people think rebuilding is just getting back what you lost. But I disagree.

True rebuilding means redefining what matters.

It means realigning your life to your values.

It means reclaiming your power — not to impress others, but to rebuild on your own terms.

Looking back, I can honestly say that losing everything stripped away what wasn't meant to last.

And what came next? That was mine — fully, truly, and deeply mine.

🔷 **Action Step**: If you're in a low moment right now, ask yourself:

"What needs to go permanently, and what do I want to rebuild with intention?"**Your Legacy Is Forged in the Fire**

Everyone loves a success story — but it's the scars that give it depth.

Legacy isn't about how smooth your journey was. It's about who you became when things didn't go to plan.

It's about whether you chose bitterness or growth.

Shame or ownership.

Silence or truth.

That car park moment? It didn't just break me. It refined me.

From that point on, everything I've built — every tool, every conversation, every deal — has come from that same place of clarity and resilience.

◈ **Action Step**: Write down the hardest moment in your business journey. What did it teach you? That lesson is part of your leadership legacy. **The Power of Owning Your Story**

For a long time, I kept that part of my story quiet. I thought it made me look weak.

But here's the thing: people connect with honesty — not polish.

And when I finally started owning the full truth, everything changed.

It opened doors.

It deepened relationships.

It gave me back my voice.

Transparency doesn't weaken your brand. It strengthens it.

Because real stories resonate. And when people see you've walked through the fire and still show up — that's leadership.**Final Thought: Empowerment Begins with One Decision**

I don't know what you're facing right now.

Maybe your business is thriving.

Maybe you're just barely holding it together.

But if you've hit that quiet moment — the one where everything feels like it's come undone — know this:

You are **not** done.

You are not broken beyond repair.

You are one decision away from rewriting your story.

Choose to rebuild.

Choose to rise.

And don't ever forget —

It's not about where you've been. It's about who you become next.

Why Most Owners Leave Money on the Table

Here's a hard truth you don't hear often enough:

Most business owners leave serious money on the table when they exit.

Not because their business isn't worth more.

But because they weren't ready — financially, strategically, or emotionally.

They didn't plan.

They didn't prepare.

And when the offer came, they took it — often with a mix of relief and exhaustion — without realising they could have achieved far more.

"Lack of preparation doesn't just slow you down — it costs you hundreds of thousands."

Let's break down the key reasons why this happens (and how to make sure it doesn't happen to you).

1. Confusing Personal Value with Market Value

You've poured years — sometimes decades — into building your business. It's natural to see it as an extension of yourself.

But buyers don't pay for your personal blood, sweat, and tears.

They pay for what the business is objectively worth to them — today and in the future.

That means you need to understand your **true market valuation**, not just what you feel it should be worth.

◈ **Action Step**: Get an independent, professional valuation 1–2 years before you plan to exit. It gives you time to close the gap between perceived and actual value.**2. Weak Financials Undermine Confidence**

You might know your numbers in your head. But if they're not clearly presented — if reports are inconsistent, bookkeeping is patchy, or adjustments aren't well explained — buyers start backing away or slashing their offers.

Buyers don't want guesswork.

They want a clear, credible financial story that supports the price tag.

◈ **Action Step**: Sit down with your accountant and clean up your last 3 years of financials. Prepare a normalised EBITDA view that removes non-recurring or discretionary costs.**3. Owner Dependence Kills Value**

If the business only works because you show up every day... that's not a business — that's a job. And buyers don't want to buy your job.

Reducing owner dependence is one of the **fastest ways to increase saleability and value**.

Build a team.

Document your systems.

Delegate authority.

Prove it runs without you.

⟐ **Action Step**: Choose one area of the business where you're still the bottleneck. Hand it over to a team member in the next 90 days and document the process.**4. No Succession Plan = Higher Risk**

A solid succession plan doesn't just prepare for exit — it increases confidence for any potential buyer. It shows the business can continue to thrive, even through change.

Without it, buyers see higher risk — and they'll lower their offer to compensate.

⟐ **Action Step**: Map your org chart. Identify who could step into key roles — and where gaps exist. Start mentoring and developing those future leaders now.**5. Emotions Sabotage Smart Decisions**

This one's big.

Many owners get emotional at the negotiation table. They rush into deals out of fatigue or fear. Or they hold out for unrealistic numbers because they're not emotionally ready to let go.

Either way, value gets lost.

Being mentally and emotionally prepared makes you clearer, calmer, and far more strategic.

⟐ **Action Step**: Spend time defining what comes after the exit. The clearer your vision for life beyond the business, the easier it becomes to negotiate without emotional noise.**6. Tax and Deal Structure Are Often Afterthoughts**

Even a great headline price can be eroded by poor deal structuring or missed tax planning.

Failing to engage your accountant and tax advisor early can cost you tens — even hundreds — of thousands.

◈ **Action Step**: Get early advice on the most tax-efficient deal structures. Understand how asset vs. share sales affect your personal outcome.

Top Reasons Money Gets Left Behind

- Incomplete accounts
- Over-reliance on one customer
- No buyer narrative
- Poor forecasting
- Misaligned expectations

Final Thought: Don't Just Sell — Strategically Exit

Leaving money on the table isn't about a bad deal — it's about a lack of preparation.

But the good news is, it's preventable.

Know your numbers.

Build a business that works without you.

Get your financials clear.

Prepare your mind, your team, and your paperwork.

Because when you take the time to exit strategically, the reward isn't just a bigger payday.

It's peace of mind.

It's pride.

And it's knowing you didn't just build a business —

you finished strong.

CHAPTER 6: Creating Buyer Appeal — Positioning, Packaging & Storytelling

What Makes Your Business Valuable — And What Doesn't

When you've built a business from scratch — or spent years pouring yourself into it — it's easy to believe every part of it must be valuable.

But here's the truth that most owners don't want to hear:

Not everything you've built adds value.

Some things are sentimental.

Some are just "how we've always done it."

Some feel important — but don't actually move the needle when it comes to what a buyer's willing to pay.

Understanding what drives value — and what doesn't — is one of the most important steps you can take to prepare for a successful exit.

Let's break it down.**What Adds Real Value to Your BusinessRobust Systems and Processes**

1.

Buyers want consistency. They want to know that if they take the reins, things will keep moving smoothly. Well-documented systems signal operational maturity — and reduce perceived risk.

◈ **Action Step**: Choose one recurring process (e.g., onboarding a client or fulfilling an order) and document it clearly. Use it as a template to build out others.**A Capable, Independent Team**

2.

A business that relies entirely on the owner doesn't look like an investment — it looks like a job. A strong team shows continuity, capability, and scalability.

◈ **Action Step**: Review your org chart. Are key roles filled with people who can lead without you? If not, start upskilling or hiring to fill those gaps.**Accurate, Transparent Financials**

3.

You might know what's going on in your head — but a buyer doesn't. Clean, clear, and consistent financial documentation builds trust and increases your credibility instantly.

◈ **Action Step**: Work with your accountant to produce a 3-year financial summary that includes normalised EBITDA and clear owner adjustments.**Loyal, Diverse Customer Base**

4.

Repeat customers and diversified income streams reduce buyer risk. Heavy reliance on one client or sector can tank value, while loyalty and breadth increase it.

◈ **Action Step**: Review your top 10 customers. What percentage of revenue do they represent? If one client makes up more than 25%, it's time to spread the risk.**A Strong Culture That Attracts and Retains Talent**

5.

Culture isn't fluffy — it's foundational. A values-driven, motivated team creates operational resilience and reduces churn — two things buyers love.

◈ **Action Step**: Ask your team what they value most about working in the business. Their answers may surprise you — and guide what to protect or enhance.**What Doesn't (Necessarily) Add ValueFancy Branding Without Substance**

1.

A slick website or shiny logo might look nice, but if it's not backed by strong delivery, it won't move the valuation dial.**Legacy Products or Services**

2.

Just because a product made you money 10 years ago doesn't mean it's valuable today. If it's not profitable or scalable anymore, it may be weighing you down.**Owner-Centric Relationships**

3.

If you're the only reason a client sticks around, that's a red flag to buyers. The business needs to have loyalty to the brand, not just to you.**Unquantifiable "Potential"**

4.

Every business has potential — but buyers pay for performance. Hopes, dreams, and "if only we had time to" don't add value unless they're supported by plans, systems, or traction.**Final Thought: Value Is in the Eye of the Buyer — So Prepare Accordingly**

It's not about what you think is valuable.

It's about what the market sees as valuable.

And that means stepping back, removing the emotion, and viewing your business with a buyer's lens.

Because when you focus on strengthening the real value drivers — and stop clinging to the things that no longer serve your future — everything becomes clearer.

Clearer business.

Clearer value.

Stronger exit.

What Buyers Really Look For (That Owners Overlook)

Most business owners think buyers are obsessed with profit. And yes — healthy financials matter.

But here's the real truth:

Buyers don't just want a profitable business. They want a transferable one.

They're looking for something they can step into confidently.

Something that runs smoothly, scales smartly, and doesn't fall apart the minute you hand over the keys.

So if you're preparing for an exit, you need to think like a buyer — not just a seller.

Here's what buyers are really looking for... and what many owners tend to overlook.**1. Transferable Value — Not Owner Reliance**

Buyers aren't buying you. They're buying the business.

If your presence is central to operations, client relationships, or decision-making, you're introducing risk — and risk reduces price.

They're asking:

"If the owner walks away, does this business still work?"

◈ **Action Step**: Start documenting your role. What decisions do you make? What relationships are dependent on you? Create a plan to transition those responsibilities to your team.**2. Strategic vs. Financial Buyers**

Not all buyers are the same. Strategic buyers might be looking for synergy, customer base expansion, or capabilities you have. Financial buyers (like private equity or individual acquirers) often want stable cash flow and growth potential.

Understanding who your buyer is helps you position your business more effectively.

◈ **Action Step**: Reflect on what type of buyer your business would appeal to — and why. Use that insight to tailor how you package your financials, growth story, and team.**3. Strong Management Team**

A capable, empowered leadership team is a magnet for buyers. It signals stability, reduces owner dependence, and shows there's operational depth beyond the founder.

Think of your team as part of your "exit asset."

◈ **Action Step**: Assess your team honestly. Who's indispensable? Who's ready for more responsibility? Consider succession training for 1–2 key roles to de-risk the business.**4. Documented Systems and Processes**

Every buyer wants to know: "How does this machine actually run?"

If your operations are intuitive but undocumented, that's a risk.

If they're clear, repeatable, and measurable? That's value.

◈ **Action Step**: Choose one critical area (e.g. sales, customer onboarding, operations) and document the step-by-step process. Store it somewhere accessible and start building a playbook.**5. Growth Potential They Can Unlock**

Buyers don't just buy the past — they invest in the future.

If you've plateaued but there's obvious room to grow (new markets, upsells, automation), that excites buyers. They see the upside they can unlock post-acquisition.

🔷 **Action Step**: Create a simple one-page growth roadmap outlining where the business could go in the next 3–5 years — even if you're not the one to do it.**6. Diversified Customer Base**

Heavy reliance on a handful of customers is a red flag. Buyers want to see stable, spread-out revenue so that losing one client doesn't jeopardize the business.

🔷 **Action Step**: Calculate what percentage of revenue your top five clients represent. If any exceed 25%, develop a plan to diversify or reduce dependency.7. **Clean, Transparent Financials**

Financial clarity builds trust. If your books are messy, it slows everything down — and makes buyers nervous.

Well-prepared financials (including normalised EBITDA) make due diligence smoother and faster, and can improve deal structure.

🔷 **Action Step**: Work with your accountant to clean up historicals and produce clear monthly P&Ls, balance sheets, and cash flow statements. Include owner adjustments and commentary where needed.**8. Emotional Readiness Matters**

Here's the part no spreadsheet can show: whether you're mentally prepared to let go.

Buyers sense hesitation. If you're clinging too tightly or aren't clear about your next chapter, it adds friction — and sometimes derails the deal altogether.

◈ **Action Step**: Journal your thoughts about life after exit. What excites you? What scares you? Start defining your post-business identity before negotiations begin.**Final Thought: Show, Don't Just Tell**

Don't just say your business is solid — prove it.

Back up every claim with evidence: systems, reports, processes, team bios, client metrics.

Buyers are looking for confidence, clarity, and upside.

And the more you make that visible, the more value you create — not just in price, but in peace of mind.

Telling Your Business Story: The Power of Positioning

Let's start with something simple but often missed:

People don't buy what you do — they buy what they believe you stand for.

And in a crowded marketplace, with noise coming from every direction, the way you position your business — the story you tell, the feeling you evoke, the space you occupy — can be the difference between being overlooked and being unforgettable.

When it comes to exit planning, your story isn't just a marketing tool.

It's a strategic asset.**Positioning Is More Than a Tagline**

Many owners think "positioning" is just branding or design. It's not.

Positioning is about clarity.

Clarity about what makes you different, who you're for, and why anyone should care.

It's what sits in the mind of your ideal client — and eventually, your ideal buyer — when they think of you.

If your story is fuzzy, generic, or trying to be everything to everyone, it becomes forgettable.

But when it's sharp, authentic, and consistent?

That's when the magic happens.**Your Unique Value Proposition: Own It**

Every business has something that sets it apart — a process, a promise, a tone, a niche, a belief system.

The problem is, most owners are too close to the day-to-day to see it clearly. What's obvious to you might be the very thing that sets your business apart to others.

◈ **Action Step**: Ask your top 3 clients or customers:

"Why did you choose us over the alternatives?"

"What do you value most about working with us?"

Look for recurring themes. That's your unique value proposition starting to speak.**Crafting a Narrative That Resonates**

Your business story isn't just the timeline of what you've done.

It's the emotional arc. The journey. The mission. The "why" behind the "what."

A well-told business story helps people connect — not just to your service, but to your purpose. And connection builds loyalty, reputation, and perceived value.

For buyers? That story helps them see the opportunity. Not just in the numbers — but in the culture, the brand, and the long-term potential.

◈ **Action Step**: Write out a short version of your business journey. Highlight:**Consistency Builds Trust — and Trust Builds Value**

- Why you started
- What problem you solve
- What you believe in
- Where the business is going next

Here's where positioning pays off: consistency.

When every part of your business — from your website, to your sales process, to your team's language — reinforces the same story, it creates coherence. And coherence builds trust.

Buyers love businesses with clarity. It reduces friction and amplifies value.

◈ **Action Step**: Audit your customer touchpoints — website, social media, proposals, invoices, team interactions. Do they all reflect the same story and tone? If not, make small tweaks to align them.**Positioning Isn't Just for Marketing — It's a Tool for Exit**

Here's what's often missed:

Great positioning doesn't just attract customers.

It attracts better buyers.

Buyers want businesses that:

- Know who they are
- Know what they stand for
- Know where they're going

When your business story is clear, you don't just increase your sale price — you reduce buyer hesitation. You show confidence, culture, and capability. That's incredibly valuable during negotiation.**Final Thought: Don't Just Tell the Story —** Live **It**

Your business positioning isn't something you write once and leave on a dusty page.

It should be lived — by you, your team, and eventually, the next owner.

So get clear on what you stand for.

Craft a message that reflects your values and direction.

And tell the story in a way only you can.

Because in the end, buyers aren't just investing in your business.

They're buying into your story.

Make it one worth remembering.

What Kind of Buyer Is Right for You?

Not all buyers are created equal.

When you're preparing to exit your business, understanding **who you're selling to** can be just as important as knowing **what you're selling**.

You see, the buyer you attract — or choose to engage with — will shape everything: your valuation, your deal structure, your legacy, and even your emotional readiness.

So let's break down the three main buyer types you'll encounter on the path to exit: **Strategic**, **Financial**, and **Successor**. Each one sees your business through a different lens — and if you understand their motivations, you can position yourself to meet them with clarity and confidence.

Buyer Type	What They Want	Red Flag for Them
Strategic	Synergies, IP, market share	Culture clash risk
Financial	EBITDA, systems, cashflow	Over-reliance on owner
Successor	Continuity, mentorship	No training plan in place

1. Strategic Buyers: Paying for Synergy, Not Just Profit

Strategic buyers are typically other companies already operating in your space — or in a complementary one. They're looking for synergies: cost savings, customer base expansion, new capabilities, or a fast way to grow their footprint.

Here's the key: **they're not just buying your cash flow — they're buying fit**. If your business plugs in neatly to their strategy, they might pay a premium.

Think: competitors, suppliers, clients, or even firms in adjacent industries.

⯑ **Action Step**: Identify 3–5 businesses that would gain a strategic advantage by acquiring you. Could they cross-sell to your clients? Enter a new region? Cut overheads by integrating ops?

Strategic buyers are most influenced by:2. Financial Buyers: Focused on the Numbers

- Market position
- Brand strength
- Customer lists
- Team capabilities
- Synergistic potential

Financial buyers include private equity firms, search funds, high-net-worth individuals, and investor groups. Their goal is simple: **generate a return**.

They're buying your future profits — not your story. They want stability, scalability, and predictable cash flow. And they'll dig deep into your numbers to get there.

This is where **clean financials, documented systems, and a solid team** become invaluable.

◈ **Action Step**: Prepare a clear normalised EBITDA view that strips out non-recurring costs and owner-specific expenses. Financial buyers will want to see true operational performance.

Financial buyers are most influenced by:3. Successor Buyers: Legacy Keepers

- Historical and projected EBITDA
- Owner independence
- Operational efficiency
- Recurring revenue
- Risk mitigation

This is the most emotionally-driven buyer type — and often overlooked.

Successor buyers can be family members, existing employees, or even a mission-aligned individual from outside the business who wants to step into your shoes. For them, it's not just about profit — it's about **continuity**.

They care about preserving culture. Protecting jobs. Carrying the torch. The downside? They may not always have the capital or deal sophistication of other buyer types.

But if legacy is a non-negotiable for you — successors can be the most rewarding exit path.

◈ **Action Step**: Consider who within (or around) your business already understands the model, cares about the mission, and might be willing to step up. A gentle conversation can open the door.

Successor buyers are most influenced by:Tailoring Your Strategy to Fit the Buyer

- Mission alignment
- Team culture
- Long-term potential
- Mentorship opportunities
- Reasonable deal terms

Once you know who you're targeting, you can tailor your entire exit prep to match.

- Strategic buyers? Highlight the synergies and expansion opportunities.
- Financial buyers? Sharpen your numbers, reduce risk, and present a strong ROI story.
- Successor buyers? Focus on culture, training, and a smooth leadership transition.

One size doesn't fit all — and trying to appeal to everyone can dilute your impact.

◈ **Action Step**: Decide which buyer type feels most aligned with your business and personal goals. Then align your exit narrative, prep materials, and structure accordingly.**Final Thought: Pick Your Buyer As Carefully As You'd Pick a Partner**

Exiting your business is one of the biggest decisions you'll ever make. It's not just about the cheque — it's about what happens next.

So take the time to understand your buyer.

Because the right buyer won't just pay well.

They'll carry your vision forward.

They'll honour what you built.

And they'll make your exit feel like a new beginning — not an ending.

Attracting the Right Buyer — and Closing with Confidence

Let's be honest — the idea of publicly listing your business for sale doesn't sit well with most owners.

It can feel like broadcasting vulnerability.

Staff might panic.

Customers get spooked.

Competitors start sniffing around.

But here's the good news:

You don't need to go public to attract the right buyer.

In fact, some of the best deals happen quietly — behind the scenes, through networks, relationships, and well-positioned introductions.

Let's talk about how to do it properly.**Step 1: Get Clear on Your Unique Value Drivers**

Before you start looking for buyers, you need to understand what you're actually offering — beyond the obvious.

What makes your business valuable?

- Is it the loyal customer base?
- A niche market position?
- Recurring revenue?

- Operational independence?
- Strong team or systems?

Buyers — especially the right ones — are looking for specific strategic or financial value. The clearer you are, the easier it is to attract them.

◈ **Action Step**: List your top five value drivers. These are the qualities that make your business attractive, sustainable, and transferable.**Step 2: Prepare the Essentials Behind the Scenes**

Just because you're not listing publicly doesn't mean you can skip prep. If anything, **private buyers need even more confidence** to engage.

Have these ready:

- Clean, up-to-date financials (with normalised EBITDA)
- A short overview deck (think: investment highlights, team, customers, systems)
- Proof of systems and operational consistency
- Organisational chart showing independence from the owner

This doesn't mean you reveal everything straight away. But having these ready helps you move fast when conversations begin.

◈ **Action Step**: Prepare a 1–2 page teaser summary — just enough to spark interest without revealing confidential details.**Step 3: Leverage Your Network Intentionally**

Most owners underestimate the power of their own network.

Accountants, lawyers, suppliers, peers, trade contacts — you might be one warm introduction away from your ideal buyer.

But you need to give people the right brief. Don't just say, "I'm thinking of selling." Instead, say:

"I'm exploring a quiet transition. Ideally to someone who values [X] and can take the business to the next level. If anyone comes to mind, I'd be happy to have a confidential conversation."

◈ **Action Step**: Identify 5 people in your network who could make introductions discreetly. Reach out personally — not by mass email.**Step 4: Use Stealth Marketing Wisely**

There are ways to put feelers out without revealing your business identity.

Some tactics:

- Work with a trusted broker under NDA with a curated list of buyers
- Create an anonymous teaser and share through vetted platforms
- Post "we're open to strategic partnerships" content on your LinkedIn
- Attend industry events and speak about growth opportunities (not your exit)

The aim is to signal opportunity without announcing a sale.

◈ **Action Step**: Draft a 1 paragraph opportunity pitch that keeps your identity private but conveys the value of what's for sale.**Step 5: Operational Readiness Is Your Silent Sales Pitch**

Nothing attracts serious buyers like a business that runs smoothly without the owner.

When they see a confident team, clear systems, and stable numbers — even in a quiet conversation — their interest grows.

You're showing, not telling.

◈ **Action Step**: Step back from one key area for 30 days. Let your team run it. Document how it goes. This not only reduces dependency but gives you proof that the business functions without you.**Final Thought: Quiet Doesn't Mean Passive**

Selling privately isn't about waiting for someone to appear.

It's about being strategic and selective.

It's about preparing properly.

And it's about crafting a story that resonates with the right buyer — one who sees the value in what you've built and wants to carry it forward.

So take your time.

Stay in control.

And remember: the best exits aren't always the loudest ones —

they're the ones done with clarity, confidence, and care.

Why Some Businesses Sell in 90 Days—and Others Sit for Years

It's the question every business owner quietly wonders:

"Why did that business sell so fast... and why am I still waiting?"

The truth? It's not luck. It's not magic.

And it's rarely about size or sector.

Some businesses move fast because they're **ready** — operationally, financially, emotionally, and strategically. Others stall because there are hidden frictions dragging everything down.

Let's break down what makes the difference — and how you can prepare your business to be one of the fast movers (not the ones that linger for years with no meaningful offers).**1. Preparation Isn't Optional — It's the Difference**

The businesses that sell in 90 days aren't always the biggest or flashiest — but they're prepared.

They've documented their systems.

They know their numbers.

They've already stepped back from day-to-day operations.

They've addressed the friction points before going to market.

Preparation de-risks the deal. And lower risk = faster decisions from buyers.

◈ **Action Step**: Conduct an internal "pre-flight check." Ask yourself:

- Are our financials clean and up to date?
- Do we have key processes documented?
- Can the team run without me?

If you hesitate on any of those, start there.**2. Strong Financials = Buyer Confidence**

Buyers want proof — not promises. If your numbers are a mess, even the most enthusiastic buyer will slow down or walk away.

Businesses that sell quickly have:

- Normalised EBITDA calculated
- Owner adjustments clearly laid out
- Forecasts supported by realistic assumptions
- No red flags hidden in the accounts

They expect scrutiny and pass with flying colours.

◈ **Action Step**: Work with your accountant to produce a 3-year financial pack. Include a normalisation schedule and monthly trends. Think like a buyer and leave no gaps.**3. The Business Can Run Without You**

This is a big one — and it's often what causes deals to drag.

If the business depends too heavily on the owner — relationships, decisions, delivery — it becomes a risk. Buyers need confidence that the wheels won't fall off once you leave.

◈ **Action Step**: Delegate one key area you still control. Let your team handle it for 60 days. Use that time to identify gaps and train accordingly. You're not just prepping the team — you're building value.**4. Positioning and Timing Matter**

Businesses that sell fast don't just wait for a buyer to find them — they position themselves intentionally.

They highlight the right value drivers.

They tailor their story to the right buyer profile.

They enter the market when conditions are favourable (not when they're desperate).

◈ **Action Step**: Create a one-page buyer profile. Who's your ideal buyer? Strategic? Financial? Successor? What would they find most valuable? Tailor your narrative accordingly.**5. Emotional Readiness Can't Be Ignored**

This one is underrated — but crucial.

If you're not truly ready to exit, buyers can feel the hesitation. You might overvalue the business. You might delay decisions. You might derail the deal without meaning to.

Owners who sell quickly are aligned — personally, financially, and emotionally.

◈ **Action Step**: Journal this prompt:

"What would life look like one year after I exit?"

Be honest. Are you ready to let go? If not, what would need to shift?**6. The Hidden Deal Killers: Legal and Tax Gaps**

Even if everything else lines up, poor tax planning or unresolved legal issues can stall a deal — or worse, kill it completely.

Smart sellers get ahead of this by working with advisors early to:

- Address share structure and liabilities
- Plan for tax efficiency
- Review contracts and compliance

◈ **Action Step**: Ask your accountant and solicitor to conduct a "readiness review." Fixing issues early can shave months off your exit timeline.**Final Thought: Deals Don't Drag — They Get Delayed by Friction**

If your business has been sitting on the market with no serious movement, something needs attention.

And if you haven't gone to market yet — this is your opportunity to prepare properly and move fast when the time is right.

Because selling in 90 days isn't about luck.

It's about clarity.

It's about readiness.

And it's about being so well prepared that the right buyer can't help but say yes.

Creating a Deal Room That Impresses Serious Buyers

Let's be blunt: when the right buyer shows up, you don't want to be scrambling.

You want to look like a business that's not just attractive — but ready.

Organised. Thoughtful. Trustworthy.

Like you've done this before... even if you haven't.

And that's where the **deal room** comes in.

A well-prepared deal room isn't just a folder of files. It's a signal.

It says: "We're serious. We're credible. We're worth what we're asking."

So let's walk through what a deal room really is — and how to build one that impresses buyers and accelerates the deal.

What Is a Deal Room, Really?

A deal room is a secure, organised digital space (often a cloud folder or data room platform) that contains all the critical documents a buyer needs to assess your business.

But more than that, it's your first real impression. It's the backstage pass.

A messy deal room says: chaos.

A clear, complete deal room says: confidence.

What Serious Buyers Want to See

Here's what needs to be inside your deal room — broken down into five core categories:**1. Financial Clarity**

This is your credibility cornerstone.

Buyers want to see:

- Last 3 years of financial statements
- Normalised EBITDA calculations
- Management accounts (monthly or quarterly)
- Forecasts with assumptions
- Breakdown of owner adjustments (personal costs, one-offs)

◈ **Action Step**: Create a single "Financial Summary" document that links to each file, explains your adjustments, and highlights key metrics. Make it easy to understand — like you're explaining it to a smart but curious outsider.**2. Legal & Compliance**

This is where buyers sniff out red flags.

Include:

- Company formation documents
- Shareholder agreements
- Intellectual property (trademarks, patents, licences)
- Key contracts (clients, suppliers, leases)
- Insurance policies and legal correspondence

◈ **Action Step**: Ask your solicitor to review your existing legal documents. Fix or flag anything that could cause delays later.**3. Operations & Systems**

Buyers love systems. They create continuity, reduce risk, and show that the business runs without you.

Include:

• Org chart

• Team roles and responsibilities

• Documented SOPs (standard operating procedures)

• KPIs or dashboards (if used internally)

• Tech stack overview

◈ **Action Step**: Choose 2–3 key operational areas and document the processes clearly. Even simple checklists help demonstrate that the business isn't dependent on tribal knowledge.**4. Strategic & Commercial**

This is where you communicate your value drivers — what makes your business special.

Include:

• A short business overview or teaser

• Market position and competitors

• Growth opportunities

• Key customer data (volume, value, churn)

• Product/service breakdown

◈ **Action Step**: Create a short "Strategic Snapshot" — a 1–2 page document that highlights why your business is valuable today, and how it could grow with the right buyer.**5. People & Succession**

Buyers want to know who's staying, who's critical, and what happens when you leave.

Include:

• Key staff bios and tenure

• Management team overview

• Employment contracts (or summaries)

• Succession or transition plan

◈ **Action Step**: Map out a simple leadership succession plan. Who could step up? What support would they need? Buyers will value the forethought.**A Deal Room Isn't Just for Buyers — It's for You Too**

The process of building a deal room forces you to clean house.

It reveals gaps. Clarifies your story.

And gives you confidence when conversations begin.

Buyers notice when you're well-prepared. It shortens due diligence, speeds up trust, and reduces renegotiation risk.**Final Thought: Don't Just Dump Files — Tell the Story**

A deal room isn't a dumping ground. It's a curated experience.

So guide buyers through it. Use summary documents. Label everything clearly. Add context where needed.

Show them you've thought it through — and make it easy for them to say yes.

The Unexpected Buyer

When most business owners think about selling, their mind goes straight to one group: competitors.

"They'll understand the business. They've got the money. They'll want the customer base. Makes sense, right?"

It's logical. But not always true.

In fact, sometimes the best buyer — the one who pays more, protects your team, and carries your legacy forward — is someone you'd never expect.

Let me tell you a story that illustrates this perfectly.**The Vendor Who Knew Exactly Who Would Buy... Until They Didn't**

I worked with a business owner recently — a sharp, thoughtful operator who'd built a solid company over 12 years. They had good turnover, a loyal client base, and a tight-knit team. But they were ready to move on.

They were convinced their only real option was a competitor.

"They know the space. They'll see the value. They'll be able to bolt it on easily," they said.

But here's the thing: competitors often come with their own baggage — aggressive terms, risk of redundancies, or a mindset of "strip it down, absorb what we want, and ditch the rest."

This particular owner didn't want that. They cared about the team. About the clients. About what they'd built. So we pressed pause and asked a different question:

"What if the right buyer isn't in your industry at all?"

Repositioning the Story

We took a hard look at the business from the outside.

Yes, it was in a specific sector — but the real strengths? They weren't industry-specific.

What stood out were:

- A high proportion of recurring revenue
- Clean, well-documented systems
- A dependable management team
- Strong client retention
- Minimal reliance on the owner

These are value drivers that appeal across the board — not just to competitors, but to private investors, search funds, and even corporate buyers looking to enter the space.

So we repositioned the narrative.

Instead of pitching a niche business to a rival, we framed it as a **scalable, systemised investment opportunity** for someone looking for cashflow and stability without starting from scratch.

Enter the Unexpected Buyer

Within weeks, we were in discussions with a private investor — not from the same industry at all, but experienced in building teams, systemising operations, and growing businesses.

They loved the recurring revenue. They saw the operational independence. And — most importantly — they didn't want to change a thing.

They offered 15% more than the owner expected.

No layoffs.

No rebrand.

Just a smooth transition and a respectful continuation.**The Lesson? Buyers Value Different Things Than You Think**

As an owner, it's easy to assume that only someone who "gets" your world will value your business.

But buyers come in all shapes — strategic, financial, successor — and each one sees opportunity differently.

Some want synergy.

Others want income.

Some want meaning and purpose.

Your job isn't to guess who it will be.

It's to prepare the business in a way that speaks clearly to its true strengths — and to stay open to who might be listening.**Practical Takeaways**

1. Reframe your buyer list. Don't limit yourself to direct competitors. Consider:

• Investors seeking stable returns

• Individuals looking for a career shift

• Suppliers or customers in adjacent spaces

• Even employees or internal successors

2. Highlight the right value drivers. Especially:

• Recurring or repeatable revenue

• Documented systems

• Team capability

• Low owner relianceThese make your business more universally appealing.

3. Tell the right story. Frame your business in a way that speaks to financial, lifestyle, and strategic benefits — not just sector-specific jargon.

4. Stay open. The buyer you imagined may not be the one who truly values what you've built. And that's not a bad thing. Sometimes the best offers come from the outside.**Final Thought: Don't Sell Short by Thinking Small**

The right buyer may not wear the same shoes you've walked in. But they may be the perfect person to walk the path forward.

Stay open. Stay strategic.

And remember: the best buyers don't just buy what you've built —

they believe in where it can go next.

CHAPTER 7: Exit Readiness — Legal, Tax & Risk Preparation

How to Uncover Hidden Risks Before a Buyer Does

"Buyers will find the cracks. The question is — do you show up ready, or get caught off guard?"

One of the quickest ways to kill a deal — or watch the value drop like a stone — is for a buyer to find a surprise you didn't know about.

A contract clause you forgot existed.

An unresolved tax issue.

A customer concentration risk that feels fine to you — but screams "fragile" to them.

The truth is, **every business has risks**. But the smart ones uncover, address, and disclose them before a buyer ever asks.

That's how you build trust.

That's how you stay in control.

And that's how you protect the deal.

Here's how to do it.**1. Start With an Internal Audit**

You don't need to wait for a buyer's due diligence to find the cracks. Run your own.

A proper internal audit should review:

- Financials and tax filings
- Employment contracts and HR policies

- Customer and supplier agreements
- Intellectual property protection
- Compliance and regulatory risks

◈ **Action Step**: Set a calendar reminder every 12 months to do a light-touch audit. If you're preparing for exit, make it a deep dive. Bring in your accountant or a trusted advisor to help spot what you've become blind to.**2. Document Everything — And Keep It Current**

Buyers want evidence that your business runs well — not just because you say so, but because your systems prove it.

Outdated files, missing agreements, undocumented processes... they erode trust. Fast.

◈ **Action Step**: Create a digital operations folder. Include key policies, process checklists, and key contracts. Update it quarterly. Think of it like your "continuity bible."**3. Know What Your Business Is Really Worth**

Misaligned expectations are one of the top reasons deals fall apart. Owners who think their business is worth £5M — when the market says £3.5M — end up disappointed, or worse, sabotaging negotiations.

Get ahead of it.

◈ **Action Step**: Commission a professional valuation — not a ballpark guess, but a real-world, sector-specific assessment that accounts for your current risks, dependencies, and cash flow profile.**4. Run a Mock Due Diligence Process**

This one separates the serious sellers from the hopeful ones.

Get a trusted third-party advisor — ideally someone who's worked on transactions — and ask them to simulate the buyer's due diligence process.

They'll think like a buyer. Ask hard questions. Spot the red flags. And give you the breathing room to fix them without deal pressure.

◈ **Action Step**: Ask your accountant or solicitor: "If you were buying my business, what would worry you?" Document their answers and start addressing them now.**5. Strengthen Relationships That Might Be Deal-Sensitive**

Buyers will always ask:

"What happens to this business if [key supplier/client/staff member] walks?"

The more reliant your business is on specific people or contracts, the more vulnerable it looks.

◈ **Action Step**: Identify your top 3 dependencies — then create a plan to either reduce, document, or strengthen those relationships. Could be a longer contract, a succession plan, or cross-training key staff.**6. Build Buyer Trust by Owning Your Weaknesses**

Here's a secret: buyers aren't scared off by risk.

They're scared off by **unknown** risk.

So be upfront. Show them you've done your homework. Highlight the issues — and the plan to manage or fix them.

It makes you look prepared. Confident. And credible.

◈ **Action Step**: Create a "Risks & Mitigations" document. One page. One column for each risk. One for what you're doing about it. Include it in your deal room when the time comes.

Common Hidden Risks

- Undefined supplier terms
- Informal director loans
- Verbal contracts with staff or clients
- Missing IP protection
- Disorganised share register

"What feels 'normal' to you may be a red flag to a buyer."

Final Thought: You Can't Fix What You Don't See

Selling your business isn't about presenting a perfect image.

It's about presenting a truthful one — backed by preparation, clarity, and a plan.

The best exits don't come from hiding your flaws.

They come from owning them — and showing a buyer you're already steps ahead.

Because in the world of deals, **certainty sells**.

Smart Tax Planning — Without Raising Eyebrows

Let's be honest: nobody wants to pay more tax than they need to.

But equally — nobody wants a letter from HMRC with the word "investigation" in it.

There's a fine line between smart planning and dodgy avoidance. And when you're preparing to exit a business, **tax matters more than ever** — because the wrong approach can erode your sale proceeds faster than you'd think.

So how do you keep more of what you've built, without overstepping the line?

Let's break it down.

Tax Area	Risk Without Planning	Benefit With Planning
Shareholding	Unexpected CGT	Potential Entrepreneurs' Relief
Business structure	Extra tax layers	Optimised for exit
Pension/family assets	Left out of deal thinking	Personal wealth protection

Tax Minimisation vs Tax Evasion: Know the Line

First things first — language matters here.

• **Tax evasion** is illegal. It involves hiding income, falsifying records, or deliberately misleading HMRC. That's not what we're talking about.

• **Tax avoidance**, while legal, often involves schemes that push the boundaries — and many have been shut down or challenged in recent years.

What we're focused on is **tax efficiency** — using the existing rules, properly, to structure things sensibly.

It's not about clever loopholes. It's about **early, proactive, transparent planning.1. Structure Your Business Correctly**

Your legal structure plays a huge role in how your business is taxed.

Is your company a sole trader setup? Limited company? Partnership? Do you have holding structures in place? Is there a group entity?

If you're approaching an exit, the structure can impact:

• Capital Gains Tax (CGT) liabilities

• Eligibility for **Business Asset Disposal Relief (BADR)**

• How shares can be transferred

• How proceeds are received (dividend vs capital gain)

◈ **Action Step**: Speak to your accountant and a tax specialist 12–24 months ahead of your planned exit. Ask: "Is my structure optimised for a future sale?"**2. Plan Ahead for Capital Gains**

Most business owners don't realise how big an impact CGT has until it's too late to do anything about it.

Right now in the UK, **Business Asset Disposal Relief** (formerly Entrepreneurs' Relief) can reduce your CGT to 14% (18% in 2026) on the first £1m of qualifying gains — but only if you meet the criteria.

That includes:

- Owning at least 5% of shares and voting rights
- Being a director or employee
- Holding for at least 2 years

Miss one of those, and you could lose the relief entirely.

◈ **Action Step**: Review your shareholder structure now. Make sure all qualifying conditions are met and will remain so up to (and beyond) the date of sale.**3. Don't Forget Retirement Planning**

One of the simplest, cleanest ways to reduce taxable profit is pension contributions.

And if you're a business owner, **you can contribute directly from your company**, reducing Corporation Tax — while securing your future income.

It's not flashy, but it's effective.

◈ **Action Step**: Ask your accountant if your current pension setup is being used to its full potential. Consider increasing company contributions in your final years before exit.**4. Use Deductions and Credits Properly**

It's easy to overlook legitimate deductions — especially when you've been focused on growth rather than detail.

Examples include:

- R&D tax credits
- Capital allowances on equipment or premises improvements
- Home office usage (if relevant)
- Staff training, wellbeing, or even electric vehicle schemes

◈ **Action Step**: Do a line-by-line review with your accountant of last year's P&L. You might be surprised what's been missed or under-claimed.**5. Don't Be Too Clever — It Backfires**

This is important: if a tax strategy sounds too good to be true, it probably is.

Buyers get nervous around overly aggressive structures or schemes. HMRC is cracking down on avoidance harder than ever. And deals often slow down — or fall apart — when tax liabilities aren't clear.

◈ **Action Step**: Prioritise clarity and compliance. Have your accountant prepare a "tax position summary" that lays out your business's obligations clearly. It builds trust during due diligence.**Final Thought: The Goal Is Retention, Not Risk**

Minimising tax isn't about "getting away" with anything. It's about **keeping more of what you've rightfully earned**, without putting your reputation or the deal at risk.

Start early. Get professional advice. Keep it clean.

Because in the end, it's not about clever tricks.

It's about **smart, ethical, strategic choices** that protect the wealth you've worked so hard to build.

"The right tax advice pays for itself — sometimes many times over."

Outdated Agreements Almost Killed the Deal

Case Study: "The Shareholder Agreement That Nearly Sank a Sale"

- Problem
- Impact
- What fixed it
- Takeaway

We were 60% through the deal.

Serious buyer. Aligned expectations. Heads of Terms signed.

Momentum was strong.

And then... everything stopped.

What caused the slowdown?

A shareholder agreement from 1999.

Yes — literally typed, printed, and filed away more than two decades ago. Never updated.

What followed was three weeks of legal chaos, urgent meetings, and the very real risk that the buyer would walk away.

We got through it — barely.

But that experience became a permanent lesson: **legal hygiene can make or break a deal.The Hidden Danger of Legacy Agreements**

In this case, the shareholder agreement didn't reflect:

- The current ownership structure
- Decision-making rights
- Profit distributions
- Buy-sell mechanisms
- Exit clauses

Worse, one of the original signatories had passed away years ago — but their name was still on the document.

The buyer's legal team flagged it immediately.

And they were right to. It created:

- Uncertainty about who could legally authorise the sale
- Potential future claims
- Concerns about operational governance

Suddenly, a clean deal became messy — fast.**What We Did (And What You Should Do Sooner)**

We halted negotiations.

Brought in legal counsel.

Engaged all shareholders to create a **new, up-to-date agreement** that matched the reality of how the business operated today.

It took time. It took uncomfortable conversations.

But once resolved, the buyer's confidence returned, and we moved forward.

The lesson?

Don't wait until a buyer's lawyer tells you your documents are outdated.

Do your own legal audit before going anywhere near the market.**Key Legal Documents That Must Be Clean**

Here's what you should be reviewing now — not later:

◈ Shareholder Agreements

• Who can approve a sale?

• Are there drag-along/tag-along clauses?

• What happens if a shareholder wants out?

◈ Articles of Association

• Do they align with current operations?

• Have any amendments been made (and properly documented)?

◈ Contracts

• Client and supplier agreements: are they current, signed, and transferable?

- Employment contracts: especially key staff
- Lease agreements: clear terms, assignability, break clauses

◈ IP and Ownership

- Who owns what?
- Is everything registered and protected properly?

◈ Board Minutes and Resolutions

- Are major decisions documented?
- Are records accessible and professionally presented?

◈ **Action Step**: Commission a legal "pre-diligence" review 6–12 months before planning to sell. Ask your solicitor to highlight outdated agreements, missing signatures, or risks that could be red-flagged by a buyer.**Legal Hygiene = Deal Confidence**

Let's be clear: legal issues don't just slow down deals — they undermine **trust.**

When a buyer sees outdated or messy documentation, they start to wonder:

- "What else hasn't been updated?"
- "What surprises are coming next?"
- "Can I rely on this owner to tell me the truth?"

You want your business to feel tight, clean, and credible.

That's what legal hygiene signals.**It's Not About Perfection — It's About Preparedness**

No buyer expects a perfect legal setup.

But they do expect clarity, consistency, and a willingness to fix issues before they become barriers.

So take a proactive stance.

Audit your legal foundation.

And get your house in order before inviting anyone to the front door.

"If it's not in writing — it doesn't exist during due diligence."

Final Thought: Old Paper, Big Problems

One outdated document nearly derailed an entire deal.

Not because of malice. Not because of fraud.

Just because **no one had looked at it in 20 years.**

And that's the point:

Buyers don't just buy your business.

They buy your preparation, your credibility, and your ability to handle the details.

So don't let old paper cause new problems.

Get ahead of it.

And step into your exit with confidence — legal and otherwise.

How to Prepare for Buyer Due Diligence

"Due diligence isn't just an audit — it's a trust test."

Here's a hard truth most owners don't fully appreciate until it's too late: **buyers don't trust the pitch — they trust the paperwork.**

That's what due diligence is all about.

When a buyer gets serious, they'll dig deep. Into your numbers. Your systems. Your contracts. Your people. Every assumption you've made about what your business is worth? They'll test it. And that's fair — because they're making a big decision.

The mistake most owners make?

They wait until the buyer is at the table to get organised.

At that point, it's rushed, reactive, and risky.

If you want to command value — and keep control — **you prepare for due diligence well before the buyer ever asks.**

Here's how to do it right.

The 3 Phases of Due Diligence: 1. Get Your Financials in Order

1. Financial
2. Operational
3. Legal & People

This is where it starts — and where many deals fall apart. Your financials must be:

- Accurate
- Transparent
- Well-organised
- Easy to explain

You should have at least **3 years** of clean, reconciled accounts. Bonus points for:

- Monthly management accounts
- Normalised EBITDA clearly documented
- Forecasts that align with past performance

◈ **Action Step**: Sit down with your accountant and walk through every line of your P&L and balance sheet. Ask them: "What would worry a buyer?"**2. Review All Legal Documentation**

Buyers will want to see that everything's in order:

- Contracts (clients, suppliers, leases)
- Shareholder agreements
- Employee contracts
- Intellectual property ownership

• Regulatory or compliance documentation

Outdated, missing, or vague paperwork raises red flags fast.

⬦ **Action Step**: Do a legal audit with your solicitor. Update anything that hasn't been touched in more than 3 years — especially shareholder agreements.**3. Identify and Resolve Red Flags Early**

Here's what buyers often flag as issues:

• Client concentration (one customer = 50% of revenue)

• Lack of formalised contracts

• Owner dependency

• Tax liabilities

• Unexplained adjustments in accounts

The goal isn't to hide these — it's to address them. Better they hear it from you first, with a solution already in place.

⬦ **Action Step**: Create a simple "Risk & Mitigation" document. One column for the risk, one for what you've done (or are doing) to fix it.**4. Document Your Business Operations**

You may know how everything runs — but a buyer doesn't. They want to see that your business can function without you at the helm.

That means:

• SOPs (standard operating procedures)

• Org charts and role descriptions

• Clear systems and workflows

• Performance metrics and KPIs

◈ **Action Step**: Start small — document one key process each week. Use screen recordings, checklists, or written SOPs. Build your "operations manual" as you go.**5. Strengthen the Team**

The more the business depends on you, the more nervous a buyer gets.

You don't need to disappear — but you do need a visible, capable team who can run the show. This includes:

• A second-in-command or general manager

• Department leads who understand the numbers

• Documented succession or training plans

◈ **Action Step**: Identify your "single points of failure" — areas where only you have the knowledge. Then start cross-training and documenting.**6. Craft Your Narrative**

Due diligence isn't just about ticking boxes — it's about telling your story through evidence. That means being able to clearly articulate:

• How the business makes money

• What makes it attractive

• Where the growth opportunities lie

• Why it's a low-risk investment

Back every claim with a document. That's what builds buyer confidence.

◈ **Action Step**: Write a short internal "business summary" — your core story in 1–2 pages. Use this to shape your conversations and prep your data room.**Final Thought: Confidence Comes from Preparation**

Buyers don't expect perfection.

But they do expect preparation.

When you walk into due diligence with everything organised, documented, and transparent — you shift the power dynamic. You build trust. You reduce negotiation tension. And you keep more control over your outcome.

So don't wait for due diligence to become urgent.

Make it part of your exit readiness now — and watch how much smoother everything becomes.

◈ **Tip box:**

"Preparation creates control. Surprises shift the power."

Customer Concentration: The Silent Exit Killer

How Much Risk Hides in Your Top 3 Clients?

When it comes to selling your business, few things will scare off a serious buyer faster than this sentence:

"One client makes up 60% of our revenue."

That's not a business — that's a dependency.

Customer concentration is one of the most overlooked risks in exit planning. And the reason it's so dangerous is because it often doesn't feel like a problem while you're still running the business.

In fact, it usually feels like a win.

You land a big contract. You build a deep relationship. The revenue's stable. You stop worrying about new business development. It feels efficient.

But here's what a buyer sees:

Risk. Leverage. Fragility.Why Buyers Panic Over Customer Concentration

Think about it from their perspective. If one or two customers make up the bulk of your revenue, then what happens if they leave?

Buyers don't want to inherit your key-person relationships and cross their fingers. They want predictable, diversified income streams. They want insulation from disruption. And when they don't see that, they start discounting value — or walking away.

In fact, high customer concentration is one of the leading reasons deals fall through or get heavily renegotiated at the eleventh hour.**When Is Customer Concentration a Problem?**

There's no universal number, but generally:

- If any single customer accounts for more than **20–25% of your revenue**, red flags start waving.

- If your **top 5 customers** make up more than **60–70%**, buyers will dig in hard during due diligence.

Even long-term contracts won't completely remove the concern. Buyers want to see depth, not just duration.**How It Impacts Your Valuation**

Let's say your business has:

- £1M in revenue

- £200K from Customer A

- £150K each from Customers B and C

- The rest from a scattered group

A buyer may apply a **risk discount** to that £500K block because losing even one of those clients would drastically affect performance. That could knock your valuation down by 10–30%, or stall the deal entirely.

Worse still, some acquirers might structure the deal with **earn-outs**, only paying the full amount if those clients stay after the sale.

So now your exit — and your payout — is riding on something you no longer control.**How to Reduce Customer Concentration (Without Losing Revenue)**

This isn't about walking away from key clients. It's about strengthening your position and broadening your base.

Here's how to start:**Segment Your Revenue**

1.

Break down your income by customer and percentage. Know your exposure.**Rank Risk by Relationship**

2.

Are key clients tied to you personally? Are contracts in place? How long have they stayed? Analyse both numbers and narrative.**Invest in Business Development**

3.

Set targets for acquiring clients in new sectors, geographies, or sizes. Build a pipeline that offsets your overreliance.**Strengthen Mid-Tier Accounts**

4.

Look at your mid-sized clients with growth potential. What would it take to increase their spend? More touchpoints? Better upsells?**Systematise Client Ownership**

5.

Remove yourself as the "face" of the client relationship. Assign account managers. Use CRM tools. Make the relationship about the business, not the owner.**Action Steps**

◈ **Customer Concentration Audit**

This month, map out your top 10 clients by revenue. What % do they each represent? Where are you overexposed?

◈ **Diversification Plan**

Choose one under-leveraged customer segment and design a small outbound campaign. Build traction there over the next 90 days.

◈ **Relationship Transfer**

Pick one key client and introduce a second point of contact from your team. Begin gradually shifting responsibility.

◈ **Talk to Your Advisor**

If you're planning to exit within 1–3 years, ask your advisor or broker to review your customer concentration and its likely impact on valuation.**Final Thought: Strength Is in the Spread**

Customer concentration may feel like loyalty. Stability. Simplicity.

But from a buyer's seat, it's risk wrapped in revenue.

Diversifying your customer base doesn't just protect your business — it protects your exit. It improves your valuation, your deal structure, and your peace of mind.

Because the goal isn't just to sell.

It's to sell **well** — and walk away knowing your success wasn't tied to just one name on an invoice.

◈ I suggest a test:

"Would the business still feel stable if your biggest client left tomorrow? If not, address it before a buyer asks."

CHAPTER 8: What Comes Next — Deal Terms, People, and Life After Exit

Anatomy of a Deal: Terms, Structure, and Strategy

Let's demystify the deal table.

When people hear "deal structure," they often picture a clean, upfront cheque. But most deals aren't like that. They're layered — part cash, part deferred, part conditional.

And if you're not familiar with these terms before you sell, they'll feel intimidating. Maybe even unfair.

But here's the truth:

The more you understand how deals are built, the more confident you'll be when the offer lands.

Let's break it down simply — no jargon, no pressure, just straight talk.

1. Price vs. Terms: Why the Headline Number Isn't Everything

Most owners fixate on the sale price.

But buyers look at structure.

It's not just how much you get — it's how and when you get it. That difference can change everything.

A £2M offer paid 100% upfront is very different from a £2.5M offer with 50% deferred over 3 years — and more risk.

2. What a Typical Deal Structure Might Include

Component	What It Means	Why It's Used
Cash at Completion	Money you get on day one	The guaranteed part
Deferred Payment	Paid in instalments post-sale	Helps cashflow, reduces buyer risk
Earnout	Extra based on future performance	Keeps seller engaged, mitigates uncertainty
Equity Roll	You keep a share post-sale	Keeps continuity, upsides future growth
Retention/ Escrow	Held back for warranty risks	Used to cover future claims

◈ **Tip:** Don't reject a structure outright. Ask what problem it's solving for the buyer — then negotiate accordingly.

3. Common Deal Risks Owners Overlook

• **Warranties and Indemnities**These are promises you're making — and they last long after the sale. Understand what you're signing.

• **Personal Guarantees**Watch out for clauses that try to hold you liable if something goes wrong post-sale.

• **Ambiguous Earnout Terms**"Revenue-based" vs. "profit-based" — it matters. Make sure the calculation is airtight.

• **Deferred Triggers That Are Vague**If future payments depend on things outside your control (like buyer performance), tread carefully.

◈ **Tip:** Don't let "just get the deal done" blind you to future risk. Clean terms today avoid legal headaches tomorrow.

4. Find the Balance Between Trust and Protection

Deals are part business, part relationship. You want to be fair — but not naive.

The best deals feel win-win — where both sides feel confident, protected, and respected.

Get solid legal advice. Ask questions. Don't be afraid to negotiate what matters.

And always come back to your personal definition of success — does the deal deliver your version of freedom?

◈ Final Thought

You don't need to be an M&A expert.

You just need to be informed enough not to be caught off guard.

Understand the structure. Ask the right questions. Protect your future.

Because this isn't just about what you're selling — it's about what you're stepping into next.

Communicating Change: Protecting People and Culture

Let's talk about what really keeps owners up at night during an exit.

It's not always the money.

It's the people.

Your team.

Your culture.

The business you built that feels like a second family.

Because once the deal is done, everything changes — and how you handle that transition will shape how you're remembered.

Why Communication Matters More Than You Think

Exit announcements land like a thunderclap.

Even if it's been on your radar for years, your team may be hearing it for the first time. And what they hear — and how they hear it — determines everything that follows.

Silence creates panic.

Clarity builds trust.

Owners Often Ask:

- When should I tell my team?

• How much should I say?

• What if they panic and leave?

Here's the answer:

Tell them when the time is right — but never too late.

And be honest without oversharing.

If you're vague, they'll write their own narrative.

If you're grounded and intentional, they'll follow your lead.

What to Say (And What Not To)

When you're ready to tell your team, focus on three things:

1. **Why this is happening** (truthfully — values, legacy, personal transition)
2. **What it means for them** (jobs, roles, leadership changes)
3. **What happens next** (timelines, transition plan)

Avoid:

◈ Making promises you can't keep

◈ Saying "nothing will change" (something always changes)

◈ Overloading them with legal or financial jargon

Aim for calm, human, and future-focused.

Protecting Culture in the Handover

Your culture is your fingerprint. It's not written in your org chart — it's felt.

It's how people treat each other.

It's how problems get solved.

It's the stuff buyers can't put in a spreadsheet.

If it matters to you, protect it intentionally.

◈ **Action Tips:**

- Document your cultural values — in your own words
- Introduce the buyer with a focus on shared values
- Stay involved (if possible) during the handover to ease the shift
- Ask the buyer to speak directly to the team's future

The Ripple Effect of Poor Communication

We've seen it happen:

– Key staff resign because they feel blindsided

– Morale drops because no one knows what's coming

– Productivity nosedives because people are distracted and fearful

– The buyer loses confidence before completion

All of this can be avoided with one good conversation.

So don't hide. Lead.

Sample Script (to adapt)

"I want to share something important. I've been planning for the future of this business — and for my own next chapter.

I've found a buyer who understands our values, respects what we've built, and wants to take things forward the right way.

This wasn't a rushed decision. It's one I've made with deep care. I'll be working closely with the new owner to ensure a smooth, respectful transition.

I'm here to answer your questions, and I want you to know — this team matters. This culture matters. And I'm committed to protecting both."

Simple. Direct. Human.

Final Thought

Selling your business doesn't mean selling out your people.

The way you communicate change is part of your legacy.

It speaks louder than the deal terms.

And it will echo long after your final day.

So speak clearly. Lead with heart. And make your exit one they'll respect — not just remember.

Life After Exit: What No One Tells You

You've signed the deal.

The money's landed.

Your calendar's clear for the first time in... decades.

Now what?

This is the part no one really talks about.

Not in the broker meetings.

Not in the press releases.

Not in the deal room.

But it's real — and it's coming.

The Quiet After the Storm

At first, there's relief.

A sense of space.

A high from crossing the finish line.

But then comes something else.

- A strange silence.
- A loss of rhythm.
- A question that echoes louder than expected: "Who am I now?"

Even if you exited on your own terms — even if it went well — the emotional whiplash can be real.

Because the business wasn't just what you did.

It was who you were.

Why the Post-Exit Dip Happens

Exiting a business is one of the biggest identity shifts a person can go through.

You've spent years being the decision-maker, the go-to, the leader.

And then... you're not.

You lose:

- Your routine
- Your built-in social network
- Your daily sense of purpose
- The constant urgency that gave each day shape

And while those were draining at times — they were also anchoring.

What to Do Before It Hits

You don't need to fear this chapter.

You just need to prepare for it.

◈ **Try these steps** before **the exit:**

1. **Design a new routine** — Something light but intentional
2. **Revisit forgotten passions** — Music, writing, building, mentoring
3. **Get around other exited founders** — People who get it
4. **Create a purpose project** — Something meaningful that keeps you growing

This doesn't need to be a "new hustle."

It just needs to give your time and energy a home.

What Owners Say (That You Might Feel Too)

"I didn't expect to feel this... unanchored."

"I thought I'd love the freedom, but I miss the fire."

"I underestimated how much the team meant to me."

"I thought I'd be excited. Instead, I feel flat."

You're not broken.

You're adjusting.

And you'll find your rhythm again — if you give yourself grace, space, and something to move toward.

Rewrite the Story

This next chapter is yours to write.

And unlike the business journey — you don't need to scale anything.

You don't need to impress anyone.

You don't need a grand plan.

You just need truth.

- What matters now?
- Who do you want to become next?
- How do you want your days to feel?

Let the answers unfold slowly.

Not everything needs to be solved by Monday.

Final Thought

Exiting your business is not the end of your story.

It's a powerful pivot.

From building for others — to building for yourself.

From constant motion — to intentional movement.

From external identity — to internal alignment.

So breathe.

You did something remarkable.

Now it's time to live the life that freedom makes possible.

Because the greatest success isn't just what you walked away with —

It's what you walk toward next.

Final Note from the Author

You've just completed a journey most never start — one that looks at exit not just as a financial event, but as a personal, strategic, and deeply human process.

If this book helped you reflect more honestly, plan more clearly, or feel more ready than you did before — then it's done its job.

Because here's what I believe:

- Exits aren't about ego.

- They're about alignment.

- And the best ones come from owners who lead the process with clarity, not pressure.

Whether your next chapter is retirement, reinvention, or simply rest... I hope you walk into it with peace, purpose, and pride in what you've built — and how you've chosen to move on.

Let's Stay Connected

If you're at the stage where you want to take the next step — or you simply want someone to talk to who understands the emotional, strategic, and practical sides of exit — I'm here.

You can reach me directly at:

ased@thinkerz.co.uk

Or visit: www.maximumvalueexit.co.uk

There you'll find free tools, checklists, resources, and an option to book a quiet, no-pressure call.

Because legacy deserves more than luck.

It deserves a plan.

And I'd be honoured to help you shape yours.

—

With respect and belief in what's next,

Ased Iqbal

Free Tools & Resources

To help you implement the ideas in this book, I've created a set of free supporting resources:

◈ Exit planning templates

◈ Legacy worksheets

◈ Deal-readiness checklists

◈ Owner self-assessments

◈ and more...

Access everything here:

◈ www.legacysecuredexit.com/resources

These tools are completely free — no signup required — and designed to help you take action with clarity and confidence.

Acknowledgements

No book is written alone.

This one was shaped through years of conversations, real-world experience, and the generosity of those who trusted me with their stories. To every business owner who shared their challenges, hopes, regrets, and lessons — thank you. Your journeys gave this book its depth and its purpose.

To the clients and colleagues who've let me walk alongside them through their exits — your courage and clarity continue to inspire me.

To my family, for their patience through the late nights and long weekends. For believing in what I was building, even when I struggled to explain it.

To the team at Bookmagic.ai for making the writing process clearer and less lonely. And to Rethink Press — I appreciate the guidance, the support, and the belief in this project.

Finally, to you — the reader.

Thank you for picking up this book. My hope is that it helps you exit on your terms, with peace of mind and your legacy intact.

— Ased Iqbal

About the Author

Ased Iqbal is an experienced business advisor, acquisitions director, and founder of Thinkerz — a consultancy focused on helping business owners prepare for high-value exits. With over 30 years in business, Ased has worked across multiple sectors and has advised on everything from strategic growth to succession planning.

Driven by a deep belief in doing things the right way, Ased created *Legacy Secured Exit* to help owners plan and exit with clarity, confidence, and peace of mind. He's passionate about legacy, aligned decisions, and empowering entrepreneurs to move forward on their own terms.

When he's not working on deals or tools, Ased enjoys quiet days, reflective thinking, and adding long-term value — one thoughtful decision at a time.

Read more at https://legacysecuredexit.com.

www.ingramcontent.com/pod-product-compliance
Lightning Source LLC
LaVergne TN
LVHW020233210926
848481LV00016B/1848
* 9 7 8 1 0 6 8 1 8 4 3 0 7 *